SEEING RAINBOWS THROUGH THE CLOUDS

Charleston, SC

www.PalmettoPublishing.com

Seeing Rainbows through the Clouds

Copyright © 2022 by Paula Marinak

All rights reserved

Paperback: 979-8-8229-0528-3

ebook: 979-8-8229-0529-0

SEEING RAINBOWS

through the Clouds

PAULA MARINAK

To Jocelyn and Leah for your
inspiration and encouragement.

To Mr. D. for your persistence and
constant belief in me.

To all my pack members, humans and dogs
alike, who stay by my side through the rain,
wait patiently with me for the clouds to break,
help me see the rainbows, and give me the
courage to share them with others.

Contents

PART 1

When Rain Blocks Out the Sun

You may not control all the events that happen to you, but you can decide not to be reduced by them. Try to be a rainbow in someone's cloud. Do not complain. Make every effort to change things you do not like. If you cannot make a change, change the way you have been thinking. You might find a new solution.

—Maya Angelou, African American author and poet, *Letter to My Daughter*

Where's a Rainbow When You Need One?

I once had a college professor who was fond of saying, "Life is not all sweet pie and roses." I had never heard that expression before, and I haven't heard it since, but I understood his point. There is more to life than all the good things that make us feel happy and hopeful. Roses often come with thorns, and we'll probably have to swallow some bitter pills before we can enjoy a bite of sweet pie. To expand on my professor's sentiment, I would offer the idea that life is not always sunshine and rainbows. Sometimes dark clouds can block the sun's light.

These dark clouds don't always have to look like the ones we find in nature. The kinds of dark clouds I'm talking about could take the form of a lost job, a broken relationship, an unexpected health problem, a global pandemic, or countless other struggles any of us might face in our lives. We may see these clouds gathering and have some time to try to prepare for the coming storm, or they may spring up with little to no warning.

Such clouds also are likely to carry heavy rain that floods our minds and spirits with doubt and leaves us feeling like everything we thought we could count on has been washed away. But if we are brave and patient enough to weather each storm and wait for the clouds to break, odds are good that a rainbow we never expected to see will come shining through, offering us a sign of hope and a promise that better days are ahead.

That sounds great, right? But what if conditions are rarely ideal to create an actual rainbow? What if you somehow miss seeing the rainbow when it appears? Where's a rainbow when you need one? As I've learned through personal experience, if conditions aren't right for a rainbow to appear on its own when you need it, you have to find ways to make a rainbow for yourself. You have to find ways to see the good in any situation. It may take a long time, and it probably won't be easy, but you have to find a way to see rainbows through the clouds. When that beautiful spectrum of light breaks through whatever dark clouds are surrounding you, every aspect of your life that it touches will start to look more hopeful. That's what happened to me.

I experienced one of these overwhelming dark-clouds-with-flooding-rains times in late 2013 and early 2014. Around the same time my sister announced that she and her husband would be starting a family, I was facing an operation that would mean that dream could never come true for me. It was the ultimate dark cloud on my horizon. No sunshine or rainbows were anywhere in sight— or so I thought. But I soon would find out that the light and hope I needed would come from the most unexpected place. I just had to keep my eyes open and look through some pretty thick clouds to see that rainbow.

Shortly before my surgery, a longtime friend stopped by my house to visit me. During our chat she suggested I write a blog as a way to keep myself mentally active while my body was healing. She understood the magnitude of the operation and thought the blog could be a way to help my mind and spirit recuperate along with my body. At first I didn't take my friend's suggestion too seriously. I didn't think I could come up with that many topics to write about, and I didn't think there would be that many people who would be interested in what I had to say. But in the days immediately following my surgery, I thought more about my friend's suggestion. Because it was on my mind so frequently, I figured somebody was trying to tell me something that was worth paying attention to. I decided to follow my friend's advice, and on January 10, 2014, I wrote my first entry for *A Rainbow In Someone's Cloud*. This was my blog inspired by a quote from one of my favorite writers, African American author and poet Maya Angelou.

As Dr. Angelou said,

You may not control all the events that happen to you, but you can decide not to be reduced by them. Try to be a rainbow in someone's cloud. Do not complain. Make every effort to change things you do not like. If you cannot make a change, change the way you have been thinking. You might find a new solution.

From my first entry, I knew I wanted my blog to be a source of hope, comfort, and inspiration for readers. No matter what topic I chose, I hoped that people would see that they could always find reasons for optimism, light, and gratitude in even the darkest, most challenging circumstances.

In the time since I started writing my blog, and even a few years prior, a handful of people I'm close to had encouraged me to tackle something even more ambitious than blogging. They wanted me to write a book. Just as with starting the blog, I was hesitant about this idea. What could I possibly write about that would fill a book? Even more than that, who would read it?

Then one day in the spring of 2021, the idea just hit me. Why not adapt my blog and create a book?

Why not take one of the darkest times in my life, along with one of the most challenging events to affect the world in recent years, and see if I could use them to help other people? Couldn't we all use a little hope, inspiration, and comfort to light our way through dark times? Don't we all occasionally feel like we are under rain clouds, and wouldn't it help to see a rainbow when we need one most?

Ironically, without one of the saddest, most difficult times in my own life—one of my darkest clouds, so to speak—this book wouldn't exist. So don't be too afraid of dark clouds and the rain they bring. They won't last forever. When the rain stops and the sun breaks through the clouds, your reward will be a beautiful rainbow that dispels the darkness and lights a new path forward. To see that rainbow, be sure to keep your head up and your eyes open and have faith.

With each rainbow you experience, you're likely to realize that you don't necessarily need to endure the rain and clouds before the rainbows come. You'll start to see them everywhere, no matter what you're doing or what season of the year it is. Yes, as you'll find out, it's even possible to see rainbows at Christmas if you just keep your eyes and your heart open for their special light and magic. As the light grows brighter in your own life, you'll probably want to share it with others who need help seeing rainbows through their own clouds. Happiness grows faster and shines brighter when it's shared, I've learned. I hope you also find that to be true.

Whether you read this book from cover to cover or one story at a time, I hope you'll turn to it whenever you need a little encouragement and inspiration. When you see rainbows through the clouds, in whatever form they appear to you, I hope you will share them with others so the light can keep shining.

Recipes for a Rainbow

Science tells us that the recipe for a rainbow includes three ingredients: fresh air, water, and sunlight. Rainbows generally form when light enters drops of water, slowing down and bending as it passes from the lighter air to the heavier water. The sunlight reflects off the inside of the water droplets, which separates the light into its different colors. When light leaves the water droplets, that makes a rainbow. Science also tells us that rainbows aren't physical things we can make or touch. Instead, they are only visible when conditions in the atmosphere are ideal and when people are in just the right place at just the right time to see them. But what if we rarely have perfect atmospheric conditions? What if, no matter how hard we try, our timing is just slightly off or we are always looking in the wrong direction? What if there is not enough sunlight or the air is too dry? What if there are too many clouds to allow us to enjoy those gorgeous colors? How can we see a rainbow then?

Ask a child what it takes to make a rainbow. You likely will get some answers that tap into the imagination, happiness, magic, and wonder that are so often a part of childhood.

When I asked my niece this question, she had recently turned five years old. The words were barely out of my mouth before she told me she would use all her crayons to draw the most beautiful rainbow ever. The rainbow would be in the prettiest blue sky with a beautiful sun. The sky also would have the puffiest white clouds, and there would be a unicorn world in them. She said she would make the greenest grass under her rainbow. Because it was the day before Easter when I asked her how she would make a rainbow, she also told me bunnies and rainbow-colored Easter eggs would be in the grass she drew.

My nephew, who was just a few months shy of turning seven at the time, took a bit longer to think about his answer. After a couple of minutes, he told me that the first three colors for his perfect rainbow would come from some of his favorite toys. The red and yellow would come from Super Mario's outfit, and the orange would come from orange LEGO bricks. Because it was Easter time, he said the green, blue, and purple would come from the grass and the Easter eggs that decorated his Easter card from his granny. On any other day, the green and blue probably would have come from Luigi's outfit in *Super Mario Bros*. The purple might have come from the Ninjalinos, who are characters in an earlier favorite cartoon, *PJ Masks*. Just a short time before the discovery of Super Mario and his friends, many of the ingredients in my nephew's rainbow recipe surely would have come from Pac-Man and the archenemy ghosts who track his every move around the maze of dots.

Inspired by the kids' responses, I decided to pose this question to other members of my family as well as friends. The answers they shared ran the gamut from practical to creative. Some were even spiritual or ethereal in nature.

My uncle in Nebraska would use a prism or other piece of beveled glass to capture nearby light and create his own rainbow. One of my former elementary school teachers said he would buy a box of Skittles and sort them by color; then he would arrange the candy into the shape of a rainbow and eat the results of his work! A dear friend from Maryland said she would combine plants, leaves, and other natural elements that have the same beautiful colors as a rainbow to make her own. Another friend said her personal rainbow would come from her faith and hope in the Lord. Still another said her six grandchildren each represent the colors of the rainbow based on different traits within their personalities and the ways they interact with the world around them. One other friend said that she would harness light from people's spiritual energies, or auras, to make her own special rainbow. She believes that each life, whether past, present, or even future, has its own unique energy that is associated with a certain color. In that way each of us has our own special light that we bring with us on our journey through life.

Where did my childhood rainbows come from? I was hardly what you'd call artistic as a little girl, so my recipe for a rainbow never would have come from anything I made on my own. I don't remember any of my drawings hanging in a place of honor on the refrigerator in my mother's kitchen. I could barely draw a decent stick figure, so there wouldn't have been much to hang. Drawing anything more complicated certainly would have required a huge amount of help from a dot-to-dot book. Even staying inside the lines on a coloring book page was sometimes a tall order. My artistic inability aside, I probably would have gotten a serious stomachache or a massive cavity long before I ever ate enough candy in one sitting to represent a respectable rainbow. Besides, my father was a dentist, so making candy rainbows and eating them never would have felt like an option, except maybe at Halloween. This means I was firmly in the realms of magic and wonder when it came to imagining the perfect ingredients for my rainbows as a little girl.

My first exposure to the magic and wonder of rainbows came when I was about seven years old, while I was watching *The Wizard of Oz* on TV for the first time. If you're like me and it's been at least three decades since you last took a trip over the rainbow, let me refresh your memory.

In the opening scene, Dorothy and her cairn terrier, Toto, are coming back from a very unsettling encounter with the town's least favorite resident, Miss Gulch. Even though Dorothy appears to be skipping cheerfully along the road home, she is very worried for her best friend's safety. She tries to tell Auntie Em, Uncle Henry, and the farmhands that Miss Gulch hit Toto over the back with a rake for getting into her garden and chasing her cat, but they brush Dorothy aside because they are busy with various chores. As Dorothy tries desperately to tell her aunt what Miss Gulch is threatening to do to Toto next time, Auntie Em cuts her niece off and says, "Find yourself a place where you won't get into any trouble."

Dejected, Dorothy turns away, knowing that her little dog is the only one who will listen to her at the moment she needs it most. "Someplace where there isn't any trouble. Do you suppose there is such a place, Toto?" she asks. "There must be. It's not a place you can get to by a boat or a train. It's far, far away...behind the moon, beyond the rain." Then the iconic song begins: "Somewhere over the rainbow..."

The Wizard of Oz has no shortage of memorable scenes. Everyone who has seen the movie surely recalls the moment when Dorothy steps cautiously from the black-and-white familiarity of her house into the Technicolor kaleidoscope that is the Land of

Oz. Even now my heart still beats just a little faster in anticipation of this moment. We also gasp in amazement as Glinda the Good Witch uses her magic powers to transfer the ruby slippers to Dorothy's feet, and we may wave happily along with the Munchkins as Dorothy and Toto take their first steps down the yellow brick road. Meeting Dorothy and Toto's traveling companions along the way to the Emerald City is another fun highlight. Last but not least, who among us fans of this movie hasn't cheered when the Wicked Witch of the West melts?

Of course, the movie has its scarier moments too. Searching for your family as a tornado is bearing down on your home and knowing you are locked out of the storm cellar certainly would scare anyone I know. When that search is not successful, imagine going back to your house to make one last-ditch attempt to find your family before the tornado strikes. Your only reward is a nasty bump on the head just before you're swept up inside a twister while you are trapped in your bedroom with your dog. This isn't what most people would call a stress-free experience either. When I first saw this movie, I also remember being more than a little afraid when the Wicked Witch appeared for the first time. She disrupted the celebration of Dorothy's arrival in Oz with her shrill cackles and her infamous threat: "I'll get you, my pretty, and your little dog too!" And who can forget that dark enchanted forest and that army of flying monkeys? They're hardly what I would call cute and cuddly.

Even with all these great scenes, not a single one of them has lived as long in my memory as hearing Dorothy sing "Over the Rainbow" for the first time. From the moment the first notes came out of her mouth, I was hooked. Was there really a place we could go where skies were always blue and every dream we could possibly imagine would come true? Was there a world where everyone was always happy—including the bluebirds—and troubles melted as easily as the lemon drop candies my mother usually carried in her purse? No wonder I always said yes whenever she asked me if I wanted one! And all we had to do to get to this magical place was wish upon a star and go to sleep? I was in.

When I watched the movie again in April 2021, something happened that I don't think ever has before—I cried as Dorothy began to sing. Seeing the sweet expression on Toto's face and the way he offered Dorothy his paw a couple of times throughout the song also made my eyes well up like they never had. For a variety of reasons these days, many of us may be longing for a place where there isn't any trouble. In that moment in the story that was unfolding on the TV screen, it was as if Toto were telling Dorothy, *I don't know if this place you're singing about is real or not, but I sure will do my very best to help you find it.*

When I see a rainbow today, I still hear Dorothy's song in my head. After struggling through a global pandemic unlike anything we've seen before, who could blame any of us for wanting to escape to a land where we believed all our troubles were far behind and only happiness lay ahead?

For the last several years, I have actually worn a rainbow almost every day. It has taken on greater meaning as time has gone by. When my assistance dog—a beautiful black Labrador retriever named Maida—passed away in early August 2016, I bought myself a Rainbow Bridge bracelet as a way to comfort myself and keep her memory and the memory of all our other family dogs alive in my heart. The bracelet is made mostly of black lava beads to represent the earth and your journey through life with your pet, but at the center are seven colored beads—one for each color found in a rainbow. Just before the red bead is a bead shaped like a paw print that is meant to signify the paw prints your dog has left on your life and in your heart—the part of the dog's spirit that will remain with you always. Immediately following the violet bead is a heart-shaped bead that signifies the piece of each human heart a dog carries with him or her on the journey over the bridge.

For those who are unfamiliar, the Rainbow Bridge symbolizes a link between heaven and earth where it is said that our beloved pets wait for us until we can be together again forever. I have always cherished each of my dogs, and I choose to believe they are waiting for me at the end of that special bridge. That would be worth more to me than any pot of gold that legend tells us to look for at the end of a rainbow. Depending on your religious beliefs, a rainbow also can serve as a visible reminder of the promise that our Creator is always with us, even as we are going through dark times in our lives. The rainbow's divine light will lead us onward to brighter days when we can't see any other way forward.

But those are other stories for other times. Today when I look at my bracelet or see a rainbow in nature, I no longer think just of an overflowing pot of treasure, a magical far-off land, a symbol of an eternal promise, or the place where my beloved pups and I will be reunited one day. Now when I see a rainbow, I also see a symbol of hope and resilience—a reminder that each of us carries our own special light that we can use to make this world a better place.

As we learn when we watch *The Wizard of Oz*, Oz is not exactly the carefree place Dorothy sings about at the start of the film. Even this magical, wondrous land has its fair share of trouble. As the story progresses, Dorothy and her friends learn that they must face their fears and overcome them if they are to have any hope of getting what they want from the wizard. In fact, when things are at their most dangerous and all hope of a "happily ever after" seems lost, the Scarecrow, the Tin Man, and the Cowardly

Lion learn that brains, a heart, and courage don't really come from someone else. Dorothy's friends had these qualities all along. They just needed the right situation to find these traits within themselves and use them, just as Dorothy had to learn for herself that her heart's desire—returning to her home—was always within her reach, as long as she was willing to believe.

In much the same way, the good things we want in life are not always going to come to us easily. If you think about how rainbows form, you'll realize we will never see them in nature without having the clouds and the rain first. Just like Dorothy, the Scarecrow, the Tin Man, and the Cowardly Lion, we probably won't be able to get what we most want in our lives without facing some very big challenges along the path toward our goal. Also, like our friends from Oz, we'll discover as we follow our own roads that it's very hard—probably impossible—to get where we really want to be on our own. Just like a rainbow would never be the same if any of its colors were missing, people would never be the same if they were forced to travel this road of life alone. We need our loved ones and friends around us for love, support, encouragement, and new ideas. Besides, the people we travel with on life's journeys may possess qualities that can help us all get closer to our individual and common goals.

It's true that Dorothy's friends didn't really need to ask a wizard in a far-off city for intelligence, bravery, or love. They had what they were looking for all along, and each of those attributes was strengthened by the challenges the group faced throughout the story and their shared desire to help Dorothy get home. Likewise, each of us probably already has at least some of the ingredients we need to achieve our own heart's desires, but I don't know anyone who can tackle a recipe that complicated alone. We need to look to others who are traveling life's road with us to find some of the ingredients we need to bring that recipe to life. While we all start out on life's path with some of what we need to chase our personal rainbows, maybe the best way to get the most out of each ingredient we have is not to keep it to ourselves but to share it with others. By doing that the light we each carry inside ourselves can shine forth through the clouds and illuminate a way forward where none seemed to exist before.

Perhaps the best recipe for a rainbow today includes ingredients such as love, compassion, courage, gratitude, different ways of thinking, and a willingness to work together and face big challenges head-on to create a brighter tomorrow for everyone. If we are willing to look inside ourselves and share some of the ingredients we have with others, maybe we ultimately will create an ever-present source of light, happiness, encouragement, and hope—a never-ending rainbow that can shine whenever and wherever it's needed. Whatever your biggest dream or goal in life, that sounds like a recipe for success.

The Deepest Cut

Unless you're a plastic surgeon like my brother-in-law, surgery probably isn't a topic you talk about a lot. In fact, I'd guess that most people would rather do just about anything to avoid even thinking about going under the knife, much less spend time talking about it. Although most of us will have surgery at least a few times in our lives, it's probably safe to say that the average person likely will spend far more time out of an operating room than in one.

Recent studies have shown that most Americans undergo about nine surgeries in their lifetimes, assuming they live to be eighty-five. By that standard I am ahead of the curve already. I've had thirteen surgeries in about four and a half decades. I certainly hope that's my final total, but I realize I could have plenty of time for that number to go up. Why have I had so many operations already? When you're born with a physical disability, surgeries can be a fact of life from the start.

I made my entrance into the world in February 1977, about two months ahead of schedule. I tipped the scales at just three pounds seven ounces and measured eighteen inches. This means I weighed about as much as a small bag of potatoes, an average bag of apples, or a laptop computer, and I was three inches longer than two brand-new, unsharpened number two pencils laid end to end.

My parents were assured that I would be fine despite my preemie size. The doctors believed I would reach the same developmental milestones as other babies; it would just take a bit longer. However, as I approached my first birthday, I still hadn't rolled over, sat up, crawled, stood, or walked on my own as babies typically do in their first year of life. My parents grew increasingly concerned. This led to a visit to my pediatrician, who recommended a series of specialized x-rays called a CT scan. Around the time I turned one, an official diagnosis was made. I had hydrocephalus.

Hydrocephalus is a neurological condition that's caused by a buildup of cerebrospinal fluid, or CSF, deep inside the brain's cavities. CSF helps cushion the brain and spinal cord to protect them from injury. It also provides nutrients to these areas of the body. However, in cases of hydrocephalus, too much of this fluid increases pressure on the brain and can cause brain damage. This can result in delayed development in babies, along with poor muscle control, coordination, and balance. In turn this can lead to difficulty walking or the inability to walk. Children with hydrocephalus also often have muscle stiffness, along with spasticity (involuntary muscle movements that could be painful) in either the arms, the legs, or both pairs of limbs.

Other physical or cognitive issues can be associated with hydrocephalus, but the symptoms I just described match my own. I have used a wheelchair since childhood, and I have never been able to stand or walk alone. I used to be able to walk short distances with help. These days taking just a few steps requires a Herculean effort from me and whichever of my parents is helping me at the time. I also need assistance with the most basic tasks, from getting into or out of bed to going to the bathroom or getting a shower. Trying to get dressed by myself would probably take hours, and I would be so sweaty by the end of the process that I would need to shower all over again. Household chores such as cleaning, doing laundry, or cooking a meal are off the table at this point, and driving has been in my rearview mirror since I got behind the wheel of an adapted van when I was sixteen.

Hydrocephalus is not a common condition. It occurs in about one or two out of every thousand births in this country, and it has no cure. The most common treatment for hydrocephalus is to perform an operation where a long, flexible tube with a valve called a shunt is placed into one side of the head. The shunt's job is to relieve pressure on the brain by ensuring that excess cerebrospinal fluid flows in the correct direction at the ideal rate. This was my first surgery, performed shortly after I turned a year old. Not long after that, I had two other surgeries to correct issues that developed after my shunt was put in. Then came a procedure to place tubes in my ears to deal with recurring ear infections. If you're keeping track, this makes four surgeries—all before starting kindergarten.

Things grew quiet for me surgically until the last two years of elementary school. I had one operation in each of those years. In fourth grade I had my tonsils and adenoids removed. Even though it was still an operation, here was something that finally made me feel just like all the other kids. My friends could relate because they had been through similar operations too. However, it wasn't long before I was reminded again just how different I was. Fifth grade brought an operation that was no small potatoes: an orthopedic surgery to release tension on a tendon in my left hip to correct issues with the way that joint was positioned and to improve my gait for the short distances I could walk with help.

After that surgery I remember wishing that I would never come to a hospital as a patient again. Even though that wish didn't come true, I did get a considerable reprieve from the scalpel. I didn't see the inside of an operating room again until the calendar turned from summer to fall in 2002. At that time, I needed surgery to reconstruct my right hip. This took place shortly after I graduated from college and before I started my first full-time job. I could find no other lesson in that timing except that I needed to be sure I put my best foot forward, so to speak, as I started that new adventure. I certainly didn't feel like I needed a second major orthopedic surgery to tell me that. At least when that operation was behind me, I could put that foot forward without feeling pain in every already difficult step. I certainly wasn't going to argue with that level of success.

After that surgical hurdle was cleared, I had my wisdom teeth extracted a few years later. Compared with most of what I had been through before, this was a serving of very small potatoes—especially for the daughter of a now retired dentist. Putting a bag of frozen peas around my lower jaw a couple of times to numb the soreness was probably the easiest recovery I've ever had. In fact, when it was over, I dared to think that maybe I was finally done with operations. But that wasn't quite true.

Fast-forward to the spring of 2015. For several years I'd had a mole on my left knee that was about the size of the eraser on one of those number two pencils I mentioned earlier. I had never worried about it before. It didn't hurt, and it didn't have any of the danger signs that doctors tell you to watch for with potential skin cancers. To the average person, it probably just looked like a bigger-than-normal freckle, if anyone noticed it at all.

One day, though, I glanced down at the mole and noticed that it seemed to be creeping ever so slightly across the surface of my knee as if it wanted to overtake the freckle that was nearby. I knew this wasn't a good sign, so I had the mole removed. The tissue was sent to a lab for testing, which is standard practice for this type of procedure. It took a couple of weeks to get the results—more than the few days I was expecting. As I was waiting, I tried to convince myself that the extra time was nothing to worry about. That showed what I knew. As it turned out, the mole that had been removed from my knee was more than a harmless megafreckle. It was a melanoma in its earliest stage.

Because the lab report showed that I had skin cancer, that meant I needed a follow-up surgery to remove more tissue from the area around where the mole had been. This was to make sure there were no other cancer cells lurking in my left knee. That procedure was different from most of the others I had had thus far. It was done under local anesthesia. This meant the surgeon numbed the area he needed to work on, but I was awake the whole time. I had every confidence I would receive the best care, but that day I learned that doctors are human too.

As I was lying on the operating table and waiting for the procedure to begin, I felt the doctor tap my left knee. I had asked him to do this to signal that he was going to give me the anesthetic. I didn't want to get startled by the needle going in and cause a problem before the surgery got underway. The injection went without issue, and after a few minutes, the surgeon started his process.

When he made his first cut, I actually felt the blade go across my skin and down into my knee. A tear fell out of my left eye, and I said as calmly as I could that I had felt him cut me. After another dose of anesthetic and a little more time waiting for it to take effect, the rest of the procedure was uneventful. I remember feeling very grateful after that was over and wishing I would never have to experience anything like it again.

As it turned out, though, my follow-up surgery after my skin cancer diagnosis was not the last time I would have to go through such a procedure. Early in the summer of 2022, I had another mole removed from my left knee that was in about the same location as the first one. Because the second mole was smaller than the previous one, I hoped it was nothing. But I knew it was better to be safe than sorry, so I had it removed. When the biopsy results came back, my hopes were not confirmed. It was a second melanoma, which meant another surgery to remove surrounding tissue and potential additional cancer cells from this area of my left knee. On the surgery day, I couldn't help having flashbacks about the earlier operation. I braced myself for the sensation of feeling that first cut again. Fortunately, my worries were for nothing. No additional cancer cells were found, and I didn't feel a thing except relief and gratitude when this operation was behind me.

Some people might think that the twelve surgeries I've described so far would've left enough scars on my body to last the rest of my life. They might even think that the initial cut I felt during the first follow-up surgery on my left knee was surely the deepest cut I had ever felt. Even though I never had another operation where I felt the surgeon's blade slicing into my skin, there was one other surgery that cut deeper than all the others combined. In a manner of speaking, it cut right to my heart.

In the fall of 2013, the time came for my annual gynecological exam. All my other checkups had been normal, and I was feeling well at the time, so I had no reason to suspect this one would be different. But as my doctor was examining me, she felt something in my abdomen. She told me she thought it was a uterine fibroid. She didn't seem too concerned, so I just did as she recommended and scheduled a follow-up appointment for an ultrasound. My doctor explained that fibroids are tumors that are usually not cancerous and that they can be quite common among women. She also said they sometimes can be treated with a relatively minor procedure to remove the fibroid and that if that option is chosen, another tumor may grow in its place.

The device used for the ultrasound looked more intimidating than how my doctor's diagnosis sounded. As the technician prepared to examine me, I worried more about the length of the probe than what the test might reveal. As it turned out, the images showed that the doctor's suspicion was correct. I had a uterine fibroid that was the size of a large navel orange. At the follow-up appointment with my gynecologist, she recommended a hysterectomy as the best treatment option.

In my heart of hearts, I had known this recommendation was possible—probably even likely—depending on what the ultrasound showed. Still, no matter how much you try to prepare yourself for certain outcomes, it's never easy to hear your worst-case scenario coming true. There is always hope that things will turn out better than you expect, right up until someone tells you there isn't.

As someone who had always imagined that my future would include a family with children—despite the difficulties I face in just getting through a typical day—this news gave me quite a jolt. After the initial shock, I pretty much went numb. I remember crying a little bit in front of the doctor, but I willed my emotional floodgates not to open completely. I didn't want to face the other patients in the waiting room with tears streaming down my face as I left the office after agreeing to the procedure, along with a consultation about the surgery.

At the consultation with the specialist whom I chose to perform my hysterectomy, he talked in more detail about the surgery and why it was the best option for me. We then scheduled the procedure for January 3, 2014. It was far from my ideal way to ring in the New Year, but I knew there was no sense dragging my feet. The longer I waited, the worse this decision would hurt, and the realization that I needed this surgery had already cut pretty deeply on its own. The only thing that kept me from being completely swallowed by my sadness was knowing that the holidays were coming. I refused to let the dark cloud that was looming on my horizon ruin one of my favorite times of the year. That year more than any other, I was going to count my blessings and be truly grateful for each one.

Thanksgiving passed as usual in 2013. The morning was spent cooking while watching the Macy's parade on TV, followed by the National Dog Show in the afternoon. Then my parents, our dogs, and I went to my sister and brother-in-law's house for a delicious dinner of turkey, stuffing, mashed potatoes, green bean casserole, and cranberry sauce. After dinner came the struggle to stay awake to watch a little football and find room in our stomachs for a sliver of pumpkin pie. By the time my parents and I—and our black Labs, Maida and Zeke—found the remaining ounces of energy we each needed to go home, I reminded myself to count blessings instead of calories before finally slipping into a turkey coma.

That Thanksgiving may have been spent like many others in recent memory, but Christmas felt a little different. My parents and I, along with Maida and Zeke, went to my sister and brother-in-law's house on the afternoon of Christmas Day to have dinner and open presents. This had become our tradition since their wedding. After dinner my sister passed gifts around to each of us. That Christmas, unlike previous ones we had spent at their house, she asked my parents and me to open one particular gift last.

As a child I probably tore through my Christmas presents at least as fast as an EF5 tornado can tear through a mobile home park. But as I grew older, I took time to appreciate each gift before placing it aside and opening the next one. Christmas of 2013 was no exception to that rule. I probably took even longer than usual to open my presents that year. In fact, I remember my sister telling me as she sat next to me on the living room couch that I might want to hurry and open my last gift, or it could ruin the surprise. I didn't realize that my father had just opened his last gift: a framed sonogram photo of his first grandchild. As my mother was opening her final gift—a diaper bag filled with supplies—I turned my attention to my special present. I carefully removed the bow and wrapping paper, took off the box lid, and folded the tissue paper back. Then I paused and rubbed my eyes because they had started to fill with tears at what I saw. My surprise gift was a white onesie with the words *I love my auntie* stitched across the front. Each letter of the message was a different color of the rainbow.

"I do?" My voice couldn't help but quiver as I asked the question. Tears began rolling down my cheeks as I turned to look at my sister. We hugged each other as tightly as we ever have. This embrace lasted for several minutes, and before I knew it, we were both crying.

On one hand, I was thrilled for my sister and her husband. I knew how much they both wanted children. Because they didn't get married until their late thirties, waiting to start a family wasn't really an option. I also was delighted to know that I was going to be an aunt and had been hoping this happy news would come sometime soon. On the other hand, at that moment it also felt like my surgeon had decided to intrude on our family's Christmas celebration and perform my hysterectomy right on that couch—without anesthesia. It made the initial cut I felt during my first melanoma follow-up surgery seem like a minor paper cut.

I'm sure my sister understood both the bitterness and the sweetness of her announcement. She knew I was happy to welcome the first little one into our family. But she also understood what I was facing and how it would change me. She realized how deeply this upcoming surgery would cut on many levels.

The simple act of opening a Christmas present made it crystal clear that I was a little more than a week away from losing more than just a couple of organs. I also would forever lose my dream of having a child of my own someday. Never would I experience any of the miraculous firsts my sister and brother-in-law would marvel at in about six months. I would never see my son or daughter's first smile. I would never hear a delighted first giggle. I would never watch in complete wonder as my baby learned to roll over, sit up, crawl, or take first steps. I would never look at that precious little face and try to figure out whose eyes or smile she had. I would never see his eyes light up as he recognized my face, and I would never hear his sweet little voice call me Mommy for the first time.

For a brief moment, I couldn't help feeling overwhelmed by all the things this operation would take from me. Where was the rainbow in this cloud? Then I realized I had just seen and touched it. The onesie that my niece or nephew would wear someday had a rainbow of words across it. In fact, the baby would be the ultimate rainbow for me in this whole situation. Holding, playing with, and loving my niece or nephew, and watching him or her grow would be a daily reminder that rainbows are always around us if only we have the courage to open our eyes and look through the rain and the clouds for the light that will come when the storm passes.

After that realization I vowed to be the best auntie ever to this child and any others who might be welcomed into our family. In the week leading up to the surgery and during my time in the hospital, I was comforted because I knew that my rainbow was waiting for me. Still, there was one more cloud—and one more cut—I would have to endure before that rainbow appeared.

The day came for me to leave the hospital after my hysterectomy. I was more than ready to go home to familiar, comfortable surroundings and be with people and dogs that I loved. I could eat delicious home-cooked meals on my mother's cheerful blue-and-white plates decorated with fruit instead of rubbery scrambled eggs or overly salty mystery meat smothered in brown gravy that was served on a cafeteria tray. I could finally truly rest and allow my body to begin to heal from this latest surgery.

As soon as I got home, Maida and Zeke came trotting into the kitchen to greet me, their eyes shining, their happy grins stretching from ear to ear, and their tails wagging as if they would never stop. Normally, nothing could overshadow the joyous greeting from my beloved Labs as they tried to figure out where I had been and why I had left them for such a long time. Likewise, nothing could put a damper on my joy at being reunited with them, except for the completely unexpected package sitting at my place on the kitchen table.

On the box was a young woman holding her newborn baby. She was gazing at that child with the same adoration and devotion that I knew would be on my sister's face when she saw her baby after he was born—or the way I had imagined looking at a child of my own someday. The box contained a lactation kit for new mothers. As soon as I saw that, it felt like someone was ripping the staples out of my latest incision with bare hands. The rest of my organs surely had fallen out, courtesy of the gaping hole I felt in my midsection.

That was the only day I can ever remember feeling glad that I use a wheelchair. I don't think my legs could have supported me after I saw that package. Between that first "special delivery" and the Pampers coupon book that came in the mail the following day, I was cut completely through. My memory of opening that sweet little onesie with its rainbow-colored message of love was the biggest thing that helped drive away these clouds that threatened to completely block out any light that was left following that surgery.

Life is full of sharp edges. Sometimes we see them coming and can somewhat prepare ourselves for the pain. Other times they feel even sharper because they are unexpected. Life's sharp edges might graze us. They only hurt briefly but still are painful enough to remind us to try to avoid such situations whenever we can. Other times a sharp edge can cut to the core. It can seem as if the bleeding will never stop. Moving forward seems impossible and unbearable because it feels as if there is nothing that is strong enough to lift us out from under our pain and help us overcome it. It's not easy dealing with this kind of cut. It truly can be life changing. When something like that happens, we have two options. We can choose to get bitter or to get better.

Bitterness may have the upper hand at first. It's easy and understandable to lash out at the unfairness of life. But if left untreated, the bitterness will fester and eat you alive from the inside out. That's why, no matter how long it takes, you have to work to get better one step at a time. With patience and care, even the deepest cuts will heal. Scars will form, but eventually, they will soften and fade. The hurt will subside, and you will remain. You will move past the pain toward a brighter, more hopeful future, thanks to a love that is powerful enough to carry you out from under the dark clouds and toward the rainbows that await.

Working like a Dog

Working like a dog—what comes to mind when you hear this phrase? If you're like me, you think of someone working tirelessly to accomplish a tough task. This task is usually something that has been put off for a long time or avoided altogether because no one wants to do it. Working like a dog means working even though you are bone tired, with no thought of stopping until you have reached your goal. Others may not even recognize or praise you for your effort. Sometimes the use of this phrase breeds resentment in the one who is doing all the work because no one else will help lighten the load. Ironically, it's because of one of my dogs that I've gained a whole new appreciation for this phrase.

About a month before my hysterectomy, the younger of our two black Labs, Zeke, had been let outside after dinner to go to the bathroom. It was mid-December, so it had already been dark for a couple of hours. Add the fact that the grass was slippery because of some recent sleet or ice that had fallen. If you think this was no ordinary bathroom trip, you're right. When Zeke came back inside, we noticed he was limping and favoring one of his hind legs. He was only about four and a half years old when this happened, so we assumed he would be OK with time, rest, and the medication his veterinarian recommended. Besides, we didn't really want to put him through another surgery at that point in his young life because he had already had more than his fair share.

Zeke's first surgery occurred when he was just six months old, and it wasn't what you might expect for a young male pup. Instead of the routine neutering procedure that usually takes place around that age, Zeke needed emergency abdominal surgery because he ate some Gorilla Glue after eating his supper. Despite a big scare for pup and people alike, Zeke made it through that surgery and recovered well. That delayed his neutering by about a month. Then he had to have two separate surgeries—one on each ear—to repair fluid-filled sacks called hematomas. They probably developed because of constant scratching related to an ear infection. After that problem was under control, Zeke's orthopedic issues, which plagued him for the rest of his life, began. He first had to have surgery on both elbows at the same time to correct moderate to severe arthritis in each joint, along with elbow dysplasia. This condition develops when the bones that make up the elbow joint don't align properly, leading to limping on a dog's front legs.

Each time Zeke faced a medical issue that required surgery, I prayed for that operation to be his last. Despite my regular prayers that Zeke would live the rest of his life free of pain and struggle, I didn't receive the answer from above that I desperately wanted after the elbow surgery. We had to deal with this latest problem instead.

A couple of weeks after Zeke slipped in the yard, his limp wasn't improving that much despite continued rest and medication. Even with my upcoming surgery, I was more concerned for my pup's well-being than my own. However, my family decided that my health had to come first since Zeke was holding his own. I couldn't drive him to the vet's office for answers myself, so I reluctantly agreed that further help for him could be put on hold.

Shortly after I got home from the hospital in early January, my family knew we had to reassess Zeke's condition. There was still no significant improvement in his ability to walk, even though it had been at least three weeks since his injury. X-rays taken by our local veterinarian showed an injury consistent with a possible torn ACL in one of Zeke's hind legs. Zeke's doctor assured us that we would not be shunned as pet parents if we waited until I had recovered a bit more from my hysterectomy before we decided how to treat this issue. But time and torn ACLs will not wait forever for anyone.

A few days after the first set of x-rays was taken, it became increasingly difficult for Zeke to walk around our house. In fact, on the Monday after I got home from the hospital, he collapsed in our front hallway downstairs. I can still hear the sickening thud his body made when it hit the floor, the noise of his nails scrabbling as he struggled to stand up again, and the sound of my father's voice as he tried to soothe Zeke and reassure him that he would be OK. In those agonizing moments, I thought I was going to have to say goodbye to my sweet little guy forever.

But he was so young that we didn't want to give up without a fight. Besides, when we had brought him home, we had promised to take care of him no matter what. We weren't about to go back on our word—especially not when we could still have so many years with him. So back he went to our veterinarian for another set of x-rays. This time a tear in his right ACL was confirmed. My father immediately took Zeke to a specialty animal hospital in the Philadelphia area for yet another operation.

Thanks to the skillful team of surgeons and repeated heavy doses of prayer from family and friends, Zeke made it through his surgery the following morning. But that was just the first step on a long, hard road to recovery. As that road stretched on, Zeke would show us exactly what *working like a dog* really meant.

The beginning stage of recovery involved encouraging Zeke to walk as much as possible inside our house. This would allow him to gradually get used to bearing weight on his legs again and to gain confidence walking in familiar and safe surroundings. Though most rooms on the first floor of our house were carpeted at the time, my parents had to buy a few long carpet runners to place down our front hallway, in the kitchen, and down the hall that leads from our kitchen to our back door. I knew Zeke was making big steps in the first part of his recovery when he got up from a long afternoon nap one day to investigate the yummy smells in the kitchen as my mother was making a chicken casserole for that night's dinner. He walked into the kitchen just as smoothly as he ever had before the injury. His eyes were bright, and his tail was wagging with every step. He was completely focused on enjoying some chicken tidbits, and he wasn't disappointed.

Having conquered walking in the house, Zeke moved on to short walks outside. The first several were with one of my parents holding a towel under Zeke's belly to prevent slipping until he got used to bearing weight on his hind legs again on the sidewalks or in the grass. Then he progressed to short walks on his leash. After a couple of weeks at that phase, Zeke started aqua therapy.

If you know anything about Labrador retrievers, you probably think Zeke would walk on an underwater treadmill with the same ease that a fish or a duck swims. Labs originally were bred to help fishermen in Newfoundland with hauling in nets and long lines. They also would dive underwater to catch cod that had slipped off fishhooks and bring it back to the boats. If a fisherman lost his hat while hauling in the day's catch, he could even count on his canine companion to jump in and retrieve that for him. These days Labs are also used as hunting dogs because of their reliability in retrieving game birds like pheasants and ducks from whatever body of water is nearby. In fact, the American Kennel Club's website describes Labrador retrievers as having a "supernatural affinity for water."

Zeke was not like a typical Lab in that way though. Unfortunately, his first exposure to water was less than ideal. Even though he was closely supervised the entire time, his head went under for a second or two. He even needed a little boost from his lifeguard to get back above the surface. Fortunately, Zeke was physically unharmed. But ever since that first dip in a pool, his fear of the wet stuff had taken hold firmly. During every other exposure to water in Zeke's lifetime, he would flail about like a drowning man if his paws couldn't touch the bottom.

This should make it easy to imagine what effort it took for both human and dog when Zeke had to do aqua therapy as part of his recovery from his elbow surgery and his ACL tear. Quite some time went by between the time my pup finished aqua therapy after his elbow surgery and the time he had to begin treatment for his torn ACL, so he was just as fearful of water during the second round of rehab as he had been during the first.

Canine aqua therapy involves having a dog walk on a treadmill in a tank of water to gradually regain range of motion and strength in the affected leg. A technician is with the dog at all times, operating the treadmill and holding a leash to make sure the dog is safe. The dog can see out of the tank on all sides, and the technician has a clear view of everything the patient is doing. However, the tank is not big enough to accommodate both a human "coach" and an adult male Labrador retriever. This meant Zeke was in the tank by himself, while my mother and Zeke's "coach," Patti, were right outside, offering praise and encouragement. For the first few treadmill sessions, Zeke's coach held a squeaky toy over one side of the tank to give him something interesting to focus on and lessen his stress about being in the water. It took a lot of time and patience, along with many treats and much praise, but Zeke eventually gained confidence and hit his stride with not so much as a whimper of distress about getting in the tank. No doubt the whimpers also were quieted by the promise of treats and a thorough rubdown when the workout was over.

That newfound confidence in the water came at just the right time. As can sometimes happen with

ACL injuries, Zeke tore his left ACL while recovering from the injury to his right side. Because his stronger left hind leg had to compensate for his weaker right side—essentially doing double duty—Zeke's left ACL eventually tore under the strain of overuse. This meant he had to undergo yet another surgery and another course of rehab.

Such a "one step forward, two steps back" turn of events might cause even the most resilient among us humans to toss our hands up in despair and throw in the towel. Not my boy though. Zeke never lost his gentle, loving spirit. He worked even harder, and we cheered him on even louder and more enthusiastically.

In round two of his recovery, Zeke actually improved to the point where he could have brief sessions walking or even swimming in chest-deep water. His rehab sessions were no longer a source of stress and fear. Quite the opposite had happened. The weekly physical therapy appointments had become a highlight. He looked forward to them the way most dogs look forward to daily walks. We would tell him, "Zeke, it's time to go see Coach Patti!" At the sound of her name, Zeke's ears would perk up, his tail would wag in anticipation, and he would cock his head from side to side as his big Labbie grin went on full display.

It was as if he were saying, *Coach Patti? She's my friend! Can we go see her now? Please, Mommy?* The shine in Zeke's eyes at the mention of Patti's name was plain to see. I'm sure he basked in the special attention she gave him. However, I also think Zeke was eager to spend time with her whenever he could because this was his way of seeing a rainbow through the clouds. He understood that Patti cared and was trying her best to help him during a very difficult time in his life. Because of that, he would do his best for her in return.

In one of those moments, I gained a new appreciation of what it really means to work like a dog. If my Zeke could keep such a happy attitude and see a rainbow through his clouds no matter how many struggles he faced, what excuse did I have for not doing the same when things got a little rough for me?

We all slip and fall sometimes when we're walking our paths through life. When that happens, it can feel stressful, scary, and even painful to get back up and keep putting one paw in front of the other. But here's some barking news. We don't have to do it alone. Motivation comes in many forms, so follow your nose and keep searching until you find what works for you. Look to those you love most for encouragement and support. Let their words fuel you to keep moving forward one step at a time. The unknown can be very frightening, but if you let go of your fear and are willing to trust, a stranger can become a most loyal friend and one of your biggest cheerleaders. Before you know it, what used to scare you will roll right off your back. Each step forward will be easier than the last, and you won't want to stop until you have reached your goal. No matter what else crosses your path, keep your eyes on the prize and never lose your enthusiasm for what you want most. Always keep love in your heart, a smile on your face, and gentleness and determination in your spirit. Above all else, just keep wagging! If you can do these things no matter what comes your way, working like a dog will always be well worth the effort.

Dream On

One piece of advice I was given for the days and weeks immediately following my hysterectomy was to rest as often as I needed to. My body had just been through major surgery at its core, and that would take time to recover. I was told from the outset that I would not bounce back from this procedure as quickly as I had from some of my earlier ones. By the time I had this operation, I was closing in on having thirty-seven candles on my birthday cake. Let's also not forget that I had already been through the majority of my 13 surgeries in that relatively short amount of time. Based on that fact alone, some people might say I had earned the right to lie down and take a nap for an hour or two if I felt like it. But I'm just not wired that way.

For as long as I can remember, I have rarely—if ever—been able to fall asleep as soon as my head hits the pillow. There might have been one time when my sister and I were younger that Mom took us to New York City for the day and we got home around two the following morning. Then I might actually have fallen asleep *before* my head hit the pillow. But that's about it. Even after a particularly busy or stressful day at work, I would guess it usually takes about ten or fifteen minutes from the time I get in bed at night until I actually fall asleep.

My doctor ordered me to take eight weeks of leave following my hysterectomy. Many people probably would look forward to having that much time to rest and relax after an operation. I wondered how long it would be before mind-numbing boredom struck. I was antsy to get back to work after just two or three weeks. During those two months or so that I was off, I only remember trying to take a nap one time. It was the day I came home from the hospital. After eating a bowl of soup for lunch, I decided I wanted to go to my bedroom and lie down. I was pretty physically and emotionally drained, so I thought sleep would come fairly easily. I couldn't have been more wrong. When my parents left after helping me get in bed, I spent some time just lying on my back and staring at the ceiling. Then I closed my eyes and tried to give myself permission to doze. I was inwardly telling myself, *Paula, you just got home from the hospital after yet another major surgery. It's OK for you to take a nap.* That approach may have helped me drift off for about five minutes before I was awake for another round of contemplating my ceiling. When that did nothing to help me fall asleep again, my inner self convinced my outer self to try counting sheep until my eyelids got too heavy to stay open. There was nothing better to do, so why not? Besides, sheep have been used to help sell mattresses in recent years, so the woolly little guys might have been able to help me relax enough to get some shut-eye. I think I got bored with that game after just two or three sheep though. But did I get bored enough to let myself take a real nap? Of course not! That would have been too easy, and those closest to me know I rarely take the easiest path toward my goal in any situation.

My next approach was to try counting how many times I breathed in one minute. Maybe by focusing on the rhythm of my breathing, I could lull myself to sleep. But I would lose count after maybe twenty or thirty seconds and have to start over. After two or three attempts at this, I realized all I was really doing was frustrating myself. That was hardly conducive to getting good rest. When mindful breathing didn't work, I decided to try counting how many times I blinked in one minute. I thought that might help my eyelids get heavier faster than trying to count a bunch of imaginary sheep. Did Wynken, Blynken, and Nod help me get to dreamland? In a word: no. Just as with the breathing experiment, I would lose count, start over, lose count again, and end up frustrated and wide awake. At that point I just lay there for a few more minutes, thinking, *Has this doctor met me? No way will I ever make it through eight weeks of this. There must be something I could be doing instead of lying here and pretending to be asleep.* That led to me giving up, getting up, and reading, watching TV, or calling someone for a chat. In later weeks I would try a bit of exercise or even log into my work email and try to catch up on that rather than revisit napping. That was just too much work.

If you also struggle with restlessness in challenging times, here's a strategy that might actually help. Consider taking lessons from a dog. Every pup who has been part of our family has elevated napping to a high art. Each one could sleep anywhere in just about any position at any time of day or night. Every dog after our first has had his or her own special sleeping spots throughout the house. Four of our girls have had their own chairs in our family room. They would be just as likely to sleep curled in a ball as flipped on their backs with their tummies on full display and their paws in the air like they just didn't care. My assistance dog, Maida, especially favored this latter posture. When our current girl, Rosie, sleeps in her chair, she alternates between sleeping in the classic ball or using the ottoman to help her stretch out more fully on her side. The first time I saw this second pose, I couldn't help but feel impressed at how clever she was!

People in our house who can't find at least one dog napping in a chair have a few other spots they might check. Our dogs might climb up on the family room sofa, claim one of the dog beds scattered throughout the house, or just stretch out on the carpet. Rosie frequently relaxes in her chair when she needs a break from chasing squirrels, taking walks, or begging for treats, but she prefers to sleep on the floor in front of the family room sofa during many evenings while my mother is reading her book or watching TV after dinner. When Rosie does this, she braces her hind legs against the couch. We think this position probably satisfies some need she has for security while she's sleeping, but we call it her "push-off mode." To us Rosie looks just like an Olympic swimmer who is about to execute the perfect flip turn off the pool wall and make the push for home in the final fifty meters.

Regardless of which position or location one of our sleeping dogs would choose, practically the only things that could rouse them from their peaceful slumbers were the crinkles of something related to food—like a lunchmeat wrapper or a potato chip bag—or the doorbell ringing if someone from UPS or FedEx was delivering a package. I have often wished I could sleep in such utter contentment and complete oblivion to whatever was going on around me.

I also will admit to being a bit envious of my dogs' tendencies to dream while they sleep. This rarely happens when I nod off, no matter how relaxed or tired I am. I've had some great examples of doggy dreamers though. When my girl Maida would flip on her back to sleep, she was so relaxed that her lips often would fall backward and show her teeth. When this happened,

Maida looked like she was smiling. This frequently made me wonder what she was dreaming about as she slept so peacefully.

Rosie also takes contented dreaming to a new level as she sometimes does something I'd never seen before she came to us. You've heard of sleep-walking, but how about sleep wagging? That's right. If Rosie is having a particularly good dream, she wags her tail while she's sleeping. Even better, she doesn't wake herself up.

Even with these two fine examples, our boy Zeke was my best subject for observing how my dogs sleep and dream. Watching him surely would have been an excellent case study to show how we should sleep and dream too. Just as I was under doctor's orders to get enough rest after my hysterectomy, the same thing was prescribed for Zeke following his orthopedic procedures. Unlike me, Mr. Zekey had no trouble following this instruction.

Dog beds are not in short supply in our home. I would wager that we have as many dog beds in our house as some people have TVs. Let's do an inventory of how many beds we had in the house during the nearly nine years Zeke was part of our family. Most of these beds are still in use today, but some are in slightly different spots from where they originally were.

To begin our count, we have a bed in the doorway between the dining room and the kitchen. As you can imagine in a house that has been home to five Labrador retrievers and one golden retriever since we moved in in December 1987, this is a prime hangout when any meal or snack is being prepared. Because I've been working from home regularly since the onset of the pandemic, the dining room/office bed also gets regular use by my favorite "supervisor."

Next, there is a bed in the family room in front of the fireplace. This gets regular use year-round, including during college sports seasons. Where else is a pup supposed to lounge while taking in the action on a college football Saturday or during March Madness? This bed also sees frequent use when I need a spotter for my workouts or when one of the dogs is relaxing with Dad—and sometimes trying to get a little snack from him—shortly before settling in for the night.

Third, in the years Zeke was with us, we had two sleeping mats stacked in the doorway between the family room and the kitchen. This arrangement became known as "the crash pad." It offered a great vantage point for seeing who was coming and going from the major areas of the house. Also, these mats were within easy distance of the front door, as well as the doors that lead from the kitchen onto the deck and the door that leads from the house to the garage. This created an ideal setup for any furry family member who happened to be on guard duty, until it became apparent that all was well and it was

OK to clock out and rest. Zeke also would crash in that spot after particularly rigorous physical therapy sessions—hence the nickname.

Fourth, when both Zeke and his great-grandmother Maida were still with us, I bought him a luxuriously velvety, super snuggly "man bed," which was kept in my parents' bedroom. Though it could only fit one of our two black Labs comfortably—and was obviously intended especially for Zeke—both dogs frequently would jockey for position in this bed at night. Zeke usually would pant frantically if Maida got in before he could claim it for himself. Then he would look to Mom or Dad to kick her out so he could settle in.

The scenario I just described makes me glad our pups had yet another sleeping option at the time. In my bedroom if you knew just where to look, you could spot a velvet-and-fleece-covered wonder with a memory foam interior that was lovingly known as "the secret bed." If my memory serves, I got this for Maida as a special present for her twelfth birthday. What else would you buy a dog who already had more toys than she knew what to do with and would get treats no matter what day it was? As fate would have it, the secret bed soon became a popular alternate spot for Zeke. After he discovered it, it was common to find him snuggled there, enjoying an afternoon nap. He positioned himself against the bolstered back as artfully as any canine catalog model could, and he never needed coaxing or direction. When Zeke saw how happy it made me to find him ensconced there, he regularly divided his sleeping time between my room and my parents' room every night.

After Zeke started spending part of the night with me, I eagerly anticipated the tip-tap of his paws down the hallway and the sound of his nose pushing my bedroom door open a little wider so he could get through. I soon found that I purposely would lie awake, waiting, until I heard him come in and start to settle in the bed before I allowed myself to drift off to sleep, often sighing as contentedly as he always did.

A summer night in July 2014 was one such occasion. I was heading down the hallway to my bedroom when Zeke came tip-tapping along behind. He walked through the doorway and made a bee-line—or as I liked to call it, a Z line—for his secret lair. By the time I had changed clothes and brushed my teeth, Zeke's deep, even breathing told me he was fast asleep. Just as I was in bed and about to drift off, I heard the sound of Zeke's toenails scratching lightly across the fabric of his bed, along with what sounded like Zeke barking in a short burst (quite furiously!) with his mouth closed. This was followed by an unbroken, low sound, which I can only assume was a dream growl. I couldn't help smiling when I heard that. Whatever he was doing in his dream, it must have been really great.

What was he up to? Perhaps he was romping freely and without pain in our backyard with his golden retriever cousins, Lucy and Penny. Maybe he was streaking off after a cat or a bunny that had dared to invade his territory. He could have been unleashing a string of canine curses on a delivery guy who had dared to approach our front door to drop off a package. As a last possibility, I imagined that Zeke had learned to read the doormat by our front door. It says, "Bark! Who goes there?" Maybe he was demanding an answer to that question in his dream.

Whatever the dream scenario, I hoped it was coming true. Many times during Zeke's waking hours, it sure seemed like he was trying his best to make the subject of his most recent dream a reality. He frequently barked at doorbells, invaders in his yard, or other perceived threats. He also would move as fast as he could to confront any approaching danger, even though I'm sure his orthopedic issues made it much harder for him to get around in the real world than in his dream world.

To paraphrase the American philosopher and poet Henry David Thoreau, we should move toward our dreams with confidence and live the best life we can imagine. Or as Aerosmith front man Steven Tyler urges us, "Dream on. Dream on. Dream on. Dream until your dreams come true."

Whether your philosophy on dreams is more literary or more rock 'n' roll, here is what I think both men were trying to say. Everyone needs dreams to provide encouragement in the face of challenges that daily life brings. Hope is one of the easiest things to give and one of the cruelest to take away. Unless a dream would harm the dreamer in some way, don't discourage it. Sometimes it's the only thing another person has to hold on to in an uncertain world. Even if the dream is not one you would follow, try to offer encouragement or support. What you give may be just the spark someone needs to get over a difficult hurdle and keep moving forward toward the goal. Because of that support, you just may get a fresh perspective and new encouragement for whatever rainbows you are chasing in your own life. So when you see your rainbow through the clouds, chase it. Don't give up, no matter how far away it seems. Put in the work to turn your dreams into action. When one dream is realized, keep chasing rainbows and dream on.

PART 2

Waiting for the Clouds to Break

A dog doesn't care if you're rich or poor, educated or illiterate, clever or dull. Give him your heart and he will give you his.

—John Grogan, best-selling author of *Marley & Me*

All his life he tried to be a good person. Many times, however, he failed. For after all, he was only human. He wasn't a dog.

—Charles Schulz, American cartoonist and creator of Snoopy and the *Peanuts* comic strip

The Weight of Waiting

Early in my childhood, I learned two very adult lessons. One was that I was and always would be very different from other people around me in ways that couldn't be missed or changed. The other was that I would have to spend a lot of time waiting. When you're born with a physical disability that requires help to accomplish anything you need or want to do—from getting out of bed, going to the bathroom, and getting dressed to picking up something you've dropped or can't reach or leaving your house to go anywhere else—waiting is something you have to learn how to do rather quickly.

My mother has always done her best to take care of my needs as soon and as well as she can. For as long as I can remember, I have never waited more than a few minutes for whatever kind of help I need. When I was a little girl, though, the wait sometimes seemed a little longer because my mother had so many demands on her time and attention. Mom didn't work outside the home after my sister and I were born. Running a house and raising two children—one of whom had special needs—along with caring for our family pets, was definitely her full-time job while my dad worked and supported our family. I'm not sure I know anyone else who could handle everything my mother has dealt with in the past four and a half decades with as much grace, skill, courage, love, and patience. I know there have been plenty of times when I haven't made her life easy. Just because I've had to spend a lot of time waiting throughout my life doesn't mean I've always been good at it.

Ironically, the first family member to teach me a lesson about patience that really stuck with me wasn't my mother. Teaching lessons in patience to her disabled daughter couldn't take precedence on her list of daily household, childcare, and pet care tasks that never seemed to end. This was something I would have to learn with time and observation. My first lesson in patience didn't come from a person at all. The task of teaching me about waiting patiently fell to our yellow Lab Sandy.

Being part of a family with two young kids, Sandy sometimes had to wait a little while longer than she might have liked for a walk, a potty break, or maybe even a meal if our parents had other things they needed to take care of first. Sandy never showed signs of stress though. She would just sit or lie down and wait patiently until Mom or Dad could take care of her. Similarly, I could always count on Sandy to help me in her own way when one of my parents couldn't come as soon as I called. When that happened, my faithful dog never failed to come lie down beside me, offering comfort and companionship until help came. Just having her close was enough to let me know that everything would be all right no matter how long it took.

Thanks to my first dog's example, I learned some valuable lessons. If there was ever something I needed that someone couldn't take care of right away, there was no need to feel stressed or sad about having to rely on someone else to come to my rescue whenever I couldn't do something for myself. I also didn't have to "bark" repeatedly until help arrived. It would be OK as long as I took some deep breaths, relaxed, and waited patiently. Most important, Sandy showed me that waiting is easier when you have a friend close by.

As I grew up, it definitely weighed more heavily on me each time I had to interrupt one of my parents, my sister, or a friend to ask for help yet again. I felt so mad at myself that I couldn't pick up the pencil I had dropped for the umpteenth time or that I couldn't grab a book, folder, or piece of paper from my backpack, which hung on the back of my wheelchair while I was in school. There were also the countless times I needed help because I couldn't reach the remote control for the TV, my book on the table nearby, my wallet or purse, or whatever else I wanted that was so close yet so far away. My body just felt so weak, so incapable, so outright useless at times when I was younger, and that scared me and made me sad. I felt like such a heavy burden to my family and friends—like deadweight that held them back from doing things they needed or wanted to do.

Of course, help still is needed with these and so many other everyday tasks. Honestly, there are plenty of days for me as an adult when those feelings from my childhood and adolescence rear their ugly heads and show that they really haven't lessened too much. Despite the physical and emotional wear and tear I surely have caused them, my family and friends have always done whatever they can for me, never wavering in their love and support.

I also have been blessed to receive the same kind of love from our furry family members. What they couldn't provide in terms of hands-on help when I needed it, every dog who has been part of our family has more than made up for with never-ending unconditional love. Each one of them has been by my side constantly through whatever clouds have come my way, doing whatever he or she can to lighten the heaviness in my heart. They have shown me that waiting does not have to feel so weighty and burdensome. It can, in fact, be a good thing. While you're waiting, you can use the time to reflect on your situation and think of ways to make it better. As the old saying goes, "Good things come to those who wait." Let's never forget that waiting is always easier when you have friends to help you pass the time who will share joyfully in the good that's to come. I dedicate this next section of stories to the companions who have always waited so faithfully with me for the rain to stop, the clouds to break, and the rainbows to come shining through. May everyone else be as lucky as I have been.

The Pack Mentality

Dogs have been part of my family for as long as I can remember. Over the years we have had five Labrador retrievers—Sandy, Snickers, Maida, Zeke, and Rosie—and a golden retriever named Sable. Since my sister left home to embark on her own life's journey, she has had two golden retrievers, Lucy and Penny, beside her most of the way. We have always considered these two "golden girls" part of our lives and hearts too. For many years after a dog first became part of our lives, I have said that if you are lucky enough to share your heart and home with at least one dog, you are no longer part of a "regular" family. You are part of something even more special. You are part of a pack. This is the story of how that pack mentality developed in our family.

The dog who left her paw prints all over my childhood was a yellow Labrador retriever named Sandy. She was everything that has always made Labs such a popular breed: smart, sweet, eager to please, loving, gentle, unfailingly patient, loyal, and beautiful. Sandy had an especially important place in my life when I was young. She was probably my first friend. Because

I was a child who was obviously different from all the other kids in the neighborhood or the classroom, other children were probably hesitant to be around me—at least until they learned that I was just like them, except that I couldn't walk or run. Sandy, on the other hand, never noticed or cared about these differences. I was just a little girl who loved her, and she was my faithful friend and companion. That was all that mattered.

Sandy was definitely more than just a dog to us. She was a member of our family. As I look back, it's fair to say that our family grew up with her as much as she grew up with us. In most of Sandy's thirteen years with us, my father's dental career was his main focus so he could provide for all of us. My mother was constantly busy as the primary caregiver to me and my sister, as well as managing all the household chores while my father was at the office. It wasn't that my mother didn't care about Sandy. It was just that my mother's daily to-do list was usually so long that our dog simply couldn't be the top priority at all times.

We all certainly loved Sandy very much. My mother always made sure she had good food and plenty of water and was walked regularly. My parents made sure she had excellent veterinary care. My sister and I played with Sandy and gave her lots of cuddles and attention. I think it's fair to say that she never wanted for anything. But as much as we loved her, Sandy was treated much more "like a dog" than any of the pups that followed her have been. For instance, Sandy always slept in the house, but she didn't sleep in one of our beds every night, which has been common with two of our dogs in recent years. Sandy was only allowed in bed on weekend mornings for snuggle sessions, which never seemed to last as long as I wanted them to. It wasn't until she got too old and too stiff in her hips to jump up—and instead slept nestled in the soft pile my comforter made on the floor after I kicked it off my bed during the night—that my parents relented and bought Sandy a dog bed of her own. Now we have enough dog beds and sleeping mats that we could put one in every major room on the main floor of our house and still probably have one or two left over. Forget shabby chic. That was so 1990s. Now we have Labbie chic!

If Sandy climbed up on the sofa or a chair in our family room in her younger years, she was usually told to get down before she could make the cushions warm. A few minutes of cuteness wasn't worth the aggravation of having to vacuum dog hair off the furniture if company was coming. When my sister and I were growing up, Mom actually preferred to keep Sandy out of the living and dining rooms when possible so her fur wasn't in every room in the house. Now our dogs have the run of the house, and we think unused rooms have no karma.

With the exception of Zeke, who had too many orthopedic issues to jump on the furniture, every dog after Sandy has had a special chair in the family room for naps. Each of Sandy's successors also has been welcome in bed no matter what time of day. Of the five dogs who have shared our lives since Sandy, my black Lab Maida slept right next to me in bed frequently, often with her head on the other pillow. Zeke alternated between sleeping next to my parents' bed and snoozing near mine in a special "man bed" of his own. As for our current pup, a yellow Lab named Rosie, she needed no encouragement at all to share a bed with her new people. Rosie has slept in bed with my mother almost every night since she came to us in the fall of 2016, and she warms up my bed most nights before I get in. Not surprisingly, it didn't take most of our dogs very long to learn that bedtime cuddles don't have to wait until the night. Our chocolate Lab, Snickers, and more recently Maida and Rosie, have each regularly joined me in bed over the years for special morning cuddle time before beginning the day. If that can't get your day off to the best start possible, I don't know what will.

Time for play is also important when you share your home with a dog. We certainly played with Sandy, but her favorite toys were tennis balls and rawhide bones. I also remember a phase my sister and I went through where we wanted Sandy to jump through our pink-and-white striped Hula-Hoop as if she were a lion in the circus. She must have thought we were out of our minds with this foolishness, but she willingly hopped through each time we asked. In contrast to the simple toys of our earlier years, now we have two large bins and an old laundry basket overflowing with squeaky toys. New catalogs come practically every time the mail is delivered. These days I easily spend as much time trying to decide what new toy to buy at Christmas or on a birthday for the pup in my life as I do deciding on just the right present for my nephew or my niece.

Just as time for play is important, you must make time for work—also known as training. We were more than willing to work with Sandy to teach her what obedience skills and tricks we could, even without help from a YouTube video. But her skills stopped at the basics, whereas future dogs learned many others. Of course, we would also reward Sandy with treats, whether a trick was involved or not. When Sandy was growing up with us, it didn't take her long to learn that Saturday mornings in our house were almost always "pancake day." Mom eventually started including a small pancake especially for Sandy as she was making all the others, hence the name.

That led to two favorite tricks in our family. One was teaching Sandy how to eat pancake bites off a fork, just like one of us would. The other was called the "nose trick," which also made its way into the repertoire of all other pups. This trick involved placing a pancake square on Sandy's nose while asking her to hold it level. After a moment or two, one of us would say "OK," and Sandy would flip the pancake piece off the tip of her nose and (usually!) catch it in her mouth. Sandy soon became pretty much automatic at this trick, even taking it to the next level with a lighter, even more tempting treat: a Cheez-It.

It took some time, but we eventually abandoned the do-it-yourself approach to dog training. After fourteen years of regularly being outsmarted by our chocolate Lab, we realized it was OK to pay for professional help to show our dog the right things to do, rather than frustrating ourselves and our pup by trying to figure out how to do that on our own. After Snickers passed away and Maida came into our family, we knew we had to change our training style. Starting with Maida, we knew we wanted our canine pupils to learn the right things to do while also socializing with other dogs. This meant that lessons at a bona fide dog training school became another change we embraced for our pups. It was just one of several other changes that would follow over the years.

It wasn't until after Sandy passed away and our golden retriever, Sable, came into our lives, soon followed by the chocolate-brown bundle of exuberance that was Snickers, that we humans finally realized how much we had changed since our time with our first dog. We were no longer just a family. We had become a pack.

If you have ever watched a nature documentary about wolves, you're probably familiar with the pack mentality. It's a term used to describe the social structure in a group of wolves that live and hunt together. The TV shows tell us that the pack mentality uses force to determine things like who is in charge and who eats first. But our dogs have always known who is in charge without vicious fights or withholding of food to get that message across. They have always felt safe and secure. They have been treated with love and respect and have known that we would provide for them and protect them no matter what. They have known from the moment they came home that they were, are, and always will be one of us.

This pack mentality may have taken about fifteen years to develop, but we are now firm believers. In fact, the toast I gave as maid of honor in my sister and brother-in-law's wedding was all about this way of thinking. It was advice from our dogs about what it takes to have a long, happy life together.

What follows is the text of this toast, along with some postwedding insight from our two most recent pack members: Penny and Rosie.

If there is one thing most people know about the Marinak family, it's that we are all dog lovers. So you could say that the celebration we are sharing in today is about welcoming a new member into our pack. Since my new brother has developed a love of dogs over the course of his relationship with my sister, I thought it most fitting this evening to offer a toast about what the six dogs that have been part of our lives could teach them about marriage and life together.

From all six dogs: It seems no accident that we so often hear dogs described as man's best friend. Each of our dogs—Sandy, Sable, Snickers, Maida, Lucy, and Zeke—has offered us unconditional friendship, acceptance, and love from the first day of joining our family. It didn't matter to them how fat or thin we were, whether we were having a good hair day, or whether our shoes matched our belts or our purses. At the end of a long day of school or work, we could feel like the top dog or the neighborhood fire hydrant. Regardless, our dogs loved us constantly and without reservation. This is the same kind of love and friendship I wish always for you.

From our yellow Lab Sandy: Be patient with each other, and always stay loyal to the ones you love. You may be asked to jump through a lot of hoops in life, whether by your partner or others. This may cause you to feel like a lion in a circus, much like Sandy may have when my sister and I went through our *Circus* *of the Stars* phase. But if you stay patient and true to each other, you can keep your focus where it should be: on the center ring, rather than the sideshows.

From our golden retriever Sable: Affectionately known as "the Laughing Dog," Sable would say you should always look for the humor in any situation. Also, never pass up a good hug, a birthday treat from Dairy Queen, or a mini doughnut (with icing and sprinkles!)—whatever the occasion for treating yourself.

From our chocolate Lab Snickers: Never back away from a challenge, even when it seems insurmountable. Sometimes you may have to think creatively to solve it, but the rewards can be great. Never lose your appreciation for the ones you love most. Whether they've been gone for five minutes or five days, always run to greet them when they arrive and never miss a chance to show your excitement at their return. And remember, a kiss on the nose is a sure way to turn aside anger.

From our black Lab Maida: Your life may not follow the path you thought it would when you started out, but have faith and do not lose heart. You will discover exactly where you are meant to be. As a good assistance dog, Maida would also tell you to recognize when you are needed and when you are not. When you are called upon to help, do so with a happy and eager heart—even if your only reward is a thank-you. Last but not least, as a mother of twenty-four who dealt with constant demands for attention, Maida would also tell you never to bark or bite when a simple growl will do.

From our black Lab Zeke: Never lose your sense of adventure and zest for life. Just beware of any sticky situations that may be lying in wait. It's all fun and games until someone ends up in a cone! When someone gives you a warning growl, respect it and back off. The situation will pass, and you will quickly be friends again. Sometimes when you don't know how to handle a tough situation, all that is really needed is to sit quietly with the one you love and offer a comforting presence.

From your golden retriever Lucy: Take time every day to play. Let your voice be heard, but recognize that the loudest voice doesn't always get the kind of attention you are hoping for. If what you want lies buried, keep digging until you find it, and try not to stress too much about the mess it creates. Last but not least, treat each other as Lucy has always treated her beloved ball. This doesn't mean you should spend all your time gnawing at each other until you are barely recognizable as the people you used to be. Instead, cherish each other, protect each other, and love each other always. And above all else, never accept any substitutes.

YEARS LATER HERE IS SOME ADVICE THAT I believe our newest pack members would have shared had they been part of that special celebration.

From your golden retriever Penny: Leaving behind everything you know to start a new life somewhere else can be very scary. But don't shy away from adventure. Trust in your pack mates, and look to them for reassurance and guidance when you need it. Remember that no matter where you walk or how far you go, you are never alone. The pack always has room for more members. Joy is all around you, so soak it up whenever you can. The more you take in, the more you can give to others. Dance your heart out whether anyone is watching or not. If others are just watching, invite them to join you. Happiness translates in any language, and enthusiasm is contagious. Most importantly, remember that you should love with your entire heart and always give even more love than you receive. That's the "golden's rule."

From our yellow Lab Rosie: Don't let bad memories and struggles from your past keep you from moving forward in search of a better life. You never know what's waiting around the corner. Have courage and take that next step. Otherwise, you could miss out on finding your true purpose in life and realizing where you are needed most. No matter who crosses your path, resist the urge to raise your hackles and scare them off without getting to know them better. Keep a kind and gentle spirit, and remember that any stranger could be a friend in waiting. Remember that those who are rescued also can be rescuers. Love freely and without reservation, no matter how much you may have been hurt before. When you find a forever love, do whatever it takes to nurture that and keep it growing. When this happens, you will do more than just take root and blossom. You will flourish, and you will reach your full potential.

BASED ON WHAT OUR DOGS HAVE TAUGHT US over the years, what nature shows portray about the pack mentality may not always be the most accurate picture. Displays of dominance are not—and never will be—what make us a pack. You won't find a fear-inducing "eat or be eaten" mindset here. To our way of thinking, a pack forms when you accept all members, including those who look different from you and see the world differently, and commit to caring for and learning from one another always. Each pack member contributes in his or her own way to help the group grow stronger. No matter how strong you get, though, don't use that strength to harm others. Only use your powers for good, and help wherever you can. When times do get tough, as they inevitably will, do whatever is necessary to help one of your own and look out for others when you can. Let love guide every choice you make. Stick together no matter what, come rain or come rainbows.

The Patchwork Puppy

Whether you are part of a pack like me or your family just includes humans, chances are you have some nicknames for one another. Because I still live with my parents, their nicknames won't be part of this story. Similarly, because I want to maintain a good relationship with my sister as well as my niece and nephew—and be more than the aunt who sends them cards with money on their birthdays and holidays—I won't mention my sister's family nickname here either. In what began as a family of four, that just leaves one of us.

My family decided to go with a rhyming scheme for the first of my nicknames that I remember, although I'm hard-pressed to think of any word that rhymes with *Paula*. My family must have been too because the first childhood nickname I recall was "Paula Walla." Eventually, that morphed into "Walskie," but I don't remember that being used very often.

Not too many nicknames were bestowed on me during my school days or into my adult life either. Other than the ones given to me by my family, the best nickname from my early years involves my favorite elementary school teacher. I remember our beloved fourth- and fifth-grade teacher, Mr. Darr, calling me "Hot Wheels." For two years he never missed a chance to greet me by that special name when he saw me, whether in his classroom or out of it. Perhaps he came up with that term of endearment as a way to boost my self-esteem since I was different from the rest of my classmates in some pretty obvious ways. Maybe he also used it as a way to encourage me to embrace these differences rather than feel self-conscious about them. Whatever his motivation, it surely worked. Hearing "How's it goin', Hot Wheels?" in his always cheerful, booming voice never failed to make me smile. Only Mr. D. could make using a wheelchair feel like a superpower any kid would be thrilled to have.

There you have a brief history of my life in nicknames. If your families are anything like mine, though, the humans are not the only members who have nicknames. The dogs do too.

Sadly, I don't think many nicknames were given to our first dog, Sandy. Two that I recall had a literary flavor to them. I remember my mother occasionally calling Sandy "Rowsby Woof" or the "Fairy Wogdog." If you're unfamiliar, these are the names of two canine characters from the children's novel *Watership Down*. It chronicles the adventures of a family of rabbits who escape the destruction of their original warren and must venture out in search of a new home.

If you think it's unusual to give a family dog a nickname from children's literature, you're probably not alone. But we had no prior experience with this, and I think we were at least original, if not widely understood. In Sandy's later years, we called her "Mellow Yellow," a nickname that was quite in keeping with her sweet-natured, always patient temperament.

It was likewise challenging to come up with nicknames for our golden retriever, Sable. She eventually became known as "Big Dog," but that was when we got our chocolate Lab puppy, Snickers, a couple of years after Sable joined our pack. This nickname came about because we thought Snickers must have viewed Sable that way. Sable's most endearing and enduring nickname was given to her by one of the children in our neighborhood. On a warm day one spring or summer, my mother was outside with Sable while talking to a neighbor across the street for a few minutes. It so happened that this neighbor's son, who was a little boy at the time, loved to hug and pet Sable whenever he saw her outside. If you've ever spent time with a golden retriever, you know this breed soaks up love and attention like there will never be enough. I have never met a golden who wasn't delighted to be on the giving or receiving end of a hug; Sable was no exception. During this particular snuggle with her buddy, Sable was perhaps panting a little harder than usual because of the heat. When the boy heard that sound, he turned to his mother and said, "Mommy, listen! She's laughing!" From that moment on, Sable was known as the Laughing Dog among our family.

When it came to nicknames for Snickers, the most frequently used one was a shortened version of her name ("Snicky") along with a few other variations. When she first came to us, Snickers also was known as "Little Brown Dog," "Little Brown," or sometimes just "Little Dog." Because she weighed ninety pounds in her prime, nicknames about her size as a pup didn't last too long. Besides shortened versions of her actual name, the other most frequently used nickname for Snickers was "Chocolate Dog." Maybe it wouldn't score points for originality, but it was accurate!

Next came our first black Lab: my girl Maida. As you can probably imagine, it was quite difficult for us to come up with a nickname for a dog whose given name was so unusual. However, one of her most common behaviors when she was excited led us to the perfect nickname for her. As many dogs do, Maida liked to walk around the house with a toy in her mouth. When she was especially pleased with whatever she was carrying, she would stand near whoever was closest and breathe very heavily while holding it. It was as if she felt extremely proud of her special prize and wanted to make sure you noticed it. Based on this sweet habit, my sister christened her "Darth Maida." As a fellow Star Wars fan, I knew that nickname was perfect the instant I heard it. However,

I couldn't help feeling a little bit disappointed in my-self for not coming up with that stroke of genius on my own.

My sister's special talent for nicknaming dogs showed itself again with her first dog, another golden retriever. Lucy was like a giant teddy bear that no one could pass by without hugging. In no time, that meant she became known as "Lucy Bear," "Baby Bear," "Golden Bear," or just "Bear."

My sister's second golden retriever, who joined her pack several years after Lucy, is named Penny. "Pretty Penny" was an obvious choice for a first nick-name because she has always been a beautiful girl. But this dog's best nickname came courtesy of my nephew just as he was learning to talk. At that time, my nephew couldn't quite pronounce the letter *n* properly. (I guess the *m* sound is easier to make when you're a little guy who's just figuring out how talking works.) So instead of "Penny," my nephew called his younger pup "Pemmy." Because my nephew pro-nounced his version of the dog's name with grow-ing confidence every time he said it, we never had the heart to correct him. "Pemmy" it became, and "Pemmy" it will forever be.

The easiest dog nicknames in the history of our pack have come with our current girl. When Rosie is the name you start with, "Rosie Posie" is a natural off-shoot. From there "Rosie Posie Pudding Pie" quick-ly followed suit. That nickname has, in turn, led to

"Pudding," as well as many others. No matter which of these terms of endearment we use—and we use them all frequently—Rosie knows they all refer to her.

Last but certainly not least on the list of nick-named pups in our pack was our boy Zeke. You'll understand in a moment why I saved him for last in this lineup, even though he's not our must recent pup. Among Zeke's several nicknames were "Zekey," "Zekey Boy," and "Zekeypants." But it's another one of his nicknames, given to him by his physical therapist, Coach Patti, that inspired the title of this story. Over the years of Zeke's treatment sessions with her, Patti eventually dubbed him "the Patchwork Puppy."

This special moniker was born in the wake of Zeke's orthopedic struggles, following his rehabil-itation from surgery to repair elbow dysplasia and after tearing both of his ACLs. In the early stages of recovery from each of these injuries, patches of fur had to be shaved from each of Zeke's legs so he could receive special laser treatments to prevent buildup of scar tissue. Electrical stimulation, or e-stim treat-ments, also were needed to help his muscles stay in good shape until he could get back on his feet and do more physical activity.

The first time I saw these patches of fur shaved off Zeke's legs, I couldn't help but feel a little sad. For one thing my boy always had one of the softest and most beautiful coats of any dog I've ever known. To see it marred in any way stung a bit, even if it was for his own good. I knew the patches would fill in with time, but the first sight of those bare spots served as one more reminder of the struggles he had endured for most of his too-short life. As time went on, I got used to the patches and became less sensitive about them. In fact, I eventually realized that each of us is probably a "patchwork puppy" in our own right.

As I came around to this new perspective, I thought about my own patchwork. The most obvious time my patchwork showed itself was when I had the surgeries for the small melanomas on my left knee. The first surgery for each of these cancers removed the patch of skin where the lesion was; the second procedure removed additional skin around the original site to make sure all the cancer was gone. Looking back even further, I see that my patchwork probably began to develop when I had my first medical procedure around the time I was just a year old. That patchwork has grown ever since. As many times as my body has been cut and stitched back together since that first surgery, some patches certainly were created along the way.

If you think about this idea in that light, there probably isn't a person among us who hasn't gotten in touch with his or her own patchwork puppy at various points throughout life. That increased self-awareness may not have come about because of surgeries though.

Consider this analogy. Each life experience can be thought of like a square in a patchwork quilt. Some are big; others are small. Some are beautiful and happy. We wish the vividness of those memories would never fade with time. We might regard other life experiences as sad and ugly. We wish we could forget them or that they had never happened in the first place. We want to leave them out of the picture, so to speak. Before you start looking for ways to cut out your own bad patches, think about this. Whether good or bad, each of these "squares" combines to create the picture of who each of us is at any point in life. That picture is rarely static. Rather, it is always changing as we have new experiences that continue to shape the overall pictures of our lives. Cutting out the "bad patches," then, can actually prevent us from recognizing pivotal events that help us grow and change into better, stronger people. We may also need the bad patches to help us appreciate the good in our lives so we can find it more easily and share it with others who may need a boost.

When you recognize patchwork in yourself and others, resist the urge to see it as undesirable or ugly. Instead, embrace the different patches that make you who you are, and extend the same kindness and grace to others.

Life may leave us feeling a bit frayed at the edges sometimes. We may even feel as if we are being torn at the seams by the circumstances we face day in and day out. Living through something as extraordinarily stressful as a pandemic surely would pull at the strongest threads binding any of us together, would it not? No matter what our situation, though, we should always be willing to put in the hard work of stitching ourselves back together as best we can. If or when we need help, we should never be afraid to ask for it. Likewise, we should not miss the opportunity to pick up the needle and thread ourselves whenever we can help someone who needs similar repair work. Expert sewing skills aren't needed, by the way. A willing hand and heart will work just fine.

Whether outwardly visible or internal, patches can be hard to get used to. It can take time to truly accept them. While you may never want others to see all your patchwork, share it with others as you feel comfortable. Doing so can help you grow, and that growth could change your life in ways you never imagined. Since you can't change the patches, maybe you can change the way you think of them and encourage others to do the same. No two patches are exactly the same. But different can be good.

No matter how many patches any of us has, they all have one thing in common. They should not be a source of sadness or shame. Everyone has them, after all. Your patches don't have to be symbols of your scars or your differences. They can combine to create a patchwork quilt of beauty, courage, strength, and resilience that represents each of us. If we only glance

quickly at all the patches, each one may look different. But if we take time to look more closely, we'll
likely find that many of these patches share some
common colors and threads. We may also realize the
patchwork quilt is bigger than we thought. Here's
even better news: there's room for more squares. A
different, even more beautiful picture emerges with
the addition of new patches. If you can share some
of that picture and the beauty of its patchwork with
others, this can be yet another way of seeing rainbows through the clouds when you need it.

Keep Calm and Paddle On

About midway through my last year of high school, members of the senior class were asked a few thought-provoking questions about their hopes for the future, with the caveat that some of the responses would be shared in the yearbook. One of those questions was: Where do you see yourself five years from now? A little more than twenty-five years have passed since that question was asked, and I'm sure I can't remember everything I said back then. My answer probably involved graduating from college with a bachelor's degree in communications and getting a job with *Sports Illustrated*—as a writer, not a swimsuit model. I envisioned myself being to the world of sports writing what Erin Andrews had become to the world of televised college football at the time.

The first part of that vision did come true, although I didn't earn my college degree until two years after the original deadline put forth in that question I answered a few months before finishing high school. The second part of that answer from my wide-eyed eighteen-year-old self wasn't even close to what actually happened and never will be. My first job after I graduated from college was to work as the associate editor of all publications produced at our state's association of school boards. As a recent college graduate, I was happy to have a job where I was actually using the degree I had worked so hard for so long to earn. However, it only took three years to realize a change was necessary.

Like many changes in life, the change in my career path came from a direction I never expected when it happened back in 2006. When I was searching for another job, a connection told me about a training program in human resources management that was available through our state's government. I had never considered a career in HR, but I was intrigued by the possibility. I went online, read about it, and decided to go through the application process. The yearlong training program was highly competitive. There were eight hundred applicants vying for just fifteen spots, and the selection process was quite rigorous. Just when I had given up hope that I would be among those chosen for this prestigious program, I got a phone call with the good news.

I marked my fifteenth anniversary with the state at the end of June 2021. There have been changes along the way, but I am happy overall. I find my career rewarding, which is a feeling that not every working person shares. Even though I have no plans to make a drastic career move between now and my retirement from my current job, I realize change can happen at any time—sometimes for reasons beyond our control. To offer just one example, life has certainly changed a lot since 2020, hasn't it? In that spirit I occasionally think about my own version of the question I was asked as my high school graduation approached. Here it is: If you had to do a job that was completely different from what you're doing right now, what would it be?

If someone told me I had to start a completely different career tomorrow, it would have to involve dogs. I also enjoy taking pictures, so why not combine two of my interests and become a dog photographer?

One photographer whose work with dogs I especially enjoy is a man named Ron Schmidt. His business, called Loose Leashes by Ron Schmidt, uses a lighthearted style to capture dogs' personalities. His photos never fail to make me smile or to change the lens through which I view certain things about life. In fact, one of his photos provided the inspiration for this story.

In 2015 I received a birthday card from my co-workers that I still have hanging on a wall of my cubicle in the office. The front of the card features a picture of a black Labrador retriever and a yellow Labrador retriever sitting next to each other in a canoe on what looks to be a lake or a river. Each dog is holding an oar in his mouth, and both are staring intently at a tennis ball that's floating enticingly a few feet in front of the boat. It's easy to see from their expressions that each one is thinking, *OK, we'll sit here calmly like this because Dad told us to. But the minute he says we can move, that ball is mine!*

This photo brings a smile to my face for many reasons every time I see it. First, it's simply a beautiful picture of a beautiful pair of dogs. Second, the dogs in this photo remind me of the black and yellow Labs that have been part of my heart for so many years and always will be. Third, I greatly admire and respect the patience, skill, trust, and hard work on the part of human and canines alike that it must have taken to capture this shot. No matter which combination of my black and yellow Labs I tried (and all would make excellent subjects!), I could promise them medium-rare New York strip steaks for dinner for a year or a lifetime of bunny-chasing privileges should any rabbit dare to hop in the direction of my mother's vegetable garden in our backyard, and I still would never come close to replicating that photo.

One day as I took a few moments to glance away from my computer screen and enjoy the picture on my old birthday card yet again, I was struck by a fourth reason to appreciate it. It dawned on me that life itself can be seen in much the same way as the photograph that Ron Schmidt captured of his two Labs sitting in a canoe and holding their oars at the ready.

This photograph is titled *The Adventurers*. To the dogs in the canoe, each new day is wide open with countless possibilities and unknowns. There are so many new places to explore and dreams to chase. Life can easily take on an adventurous flavor. While a pair of Labrador retrievers certainly could be willing to jump headlong into unfamiliar water, whether for the sake of exploring or to recapture a favorite toy, we humans might not be quite so willing to dive right in. The prospect of adventure can make people feel a combination of fear and excitement. Whether the adventure is a first day of school, a first day at a new job, moving away from home, changing careers, or anything else you can think of, it is impossible to know what awaits us before we start our journeys of self-discovery.

Whether we are facing our first time or our twenty-first time pushing off from the safety of a familiar shore and paddling into the unknown, we probably feel at least a little uncertainty about what lies ahead in the open water that seems to stretch on with no end. In my experience, there are usually two reasons why we leave the riverbank and row out into uncharted waters despite our fears. One is because challenges are easier to face when we have a beloved and trusted companion by our side to help us along the way. The second reason is that our ultimate goals are bigger than our fears. Whatever we have our eyes on is worth the effort it will take to overcome obstacles that may arise as we paddle forward to reach it.

If we think of life as a river, sometimes the water that carries our canoes toward our goals will be as smooth as glass—not a ripple or a wave in sight as we row toward the object of our desire. We may reach what we want in record time, without even breaking a sweat from our work. Other times the water could be quite choppy, the current very strong. Like the tennis ball in the photo of the Labs in the canoe, our goal may be tantalizingly in front of us. With just one more stroke, we'll have it. Sometimes, though, what we want may bob out of reach at the last second, pushing us onward and sharpening our focus as we go. Still another possibility can occur if you are alone in your canoe. You may spend some time paddling in circles because it's tough to keep your balance and manage both oars alone. You may even get stuck from time to time because your canoe runs into some mud, rocks, or other debris. However, if you share your canoe with someone who is willing to pick up an oar and help you paddle, no challenges you encounter on the river seem quite as daunting.

If you are lucky enough to have already found your paddling partner, cheers to you both! Still, even if you have found that special person, be careful not to be lulled to sleep by the comfortable rhythm you have developed with each other. Life is not always a lazy river that you can float on peacefully until you reach your destination. You never know what you'll find around the next bend. Sometimes rapids catch you by surprise. You may need to paddle pretty hard without much warning. With teamwork, courage, and a calm demeanor in the face of pressure, you can find your way back to smoother waters.

Paddling partners certainly can make life's adventures easier to navigate. Not everyone has someone by his or her side all the time though. Whether that is by choice or circumstance, traveling alone on the river of life can be a tough task sometimes. If your travels bring you in contact with a solo paddler who is struggling, consider how you might lend a hand to make that person's journey easier. If you expect to paddle with the same partner for years to come, think about ways that you can work together to reach your goals—whether individual or shared—and keep the adventure alive while still maintaining a relatively even keel. Above all else remember this: no matter how the current changes or what may cross your path as you row along the river, just keep calm and paddle on—and always keep your eye on the ball.

Twists of Fate

Going on walks with my dogs has always been a favorite pastime. From the time I was in early elementary school, I can remember my mother pushing me around our neighborhood in my first wheelchair as I held our yellow Lab Sandy's leash in my hand. I was always so happy to have my furry friend with me, and I felt like I was doing such a big, important job walking her.

In the years that our chocolate Lab, Snickers, was part of our pack, those feelings of happiness about my important job grew even stronger. By the time we got Snickers, I was fourteen and had just started high school a few months before. Earlier that year my family and I decided that I should get a power wheelchair so that I could have more independence at that stage of my life, instead of always having to rely on someone else to help me get wherever I needed or wanted to go. I had several months to get used to handling my new wheels before Snickers arrived. By the time she was ready to start exploring the great outdoors on walks, I was ready and willing to go with her.

The great outdoors may have been limited to various prime sniffing spots around our neighborhood and nearby areas, but that didn't matter to Snickers or to me. My feelings of responsibility and independence skyrocketed. Here I was, walking my pup just like every other dog owner in the neighborhood. Even though I had to rely on a wheelchair instead of my own legs to take her, Snickers always barked with unceasing eagerness whenever I asked her if she wanted to go for a walk. I needed no further proof that she looked forward to our outings and enjoyed them as much as I did—maybe even more.

The feeling that every walk was an adventure may have started with Snickers, but it grew even stronger with my black Lab Maida. Maida was the same breed as most of our other dogs, but there was one special way in which she was unlike any other pup we had known at that or any other time. Maida was a fully trained and certified assistance dog. Before joining our pack, she had been paired with a man who had rheumatoid arthritis. When that placement didn't work out, she found her way to us through a connection my father had. We were ready and willing to open our hearts and homes to a new dog, and Maida needed a new forever home. During our first meeting, it was clear a match was in the making. Home she came shortly after that.

Maida's "superpowers," as I called the skills she had learned through her specialized assistance dog training, weren't the only things that made her different from her predecessors. All our previous pups had become part of the family when they were just eight weeks old. Maida, on the other hand, came to us shortly before she turned six years old. While I felt a little sad to have missed the fun and excitement of the puppy stage of her life, I figured the trade-off would be worth it. Maida was so calm and gentle. She was also so well trained that, as one friend put it, Maida was practically "preprogrammed." Besides that, she already had some experience around people in wheelchairs because of the special training she had received. Walking her surely would be a breeze.

For the most part, that thought would prove to be correct throughout our years together. However, on our first walk, I learned that even dogs with superpowers can have moments where the cape comes off and they act just like any other dog. On my first outing with Maida, it was decided that I would use my manual wheelchair and that Dad would chauffer us around the neighborhood. This was mainly because Maida had just moved into another home. She had to get used to new surroundings, new people, and new daily routines. That was a lot to ask of a pup. Adding a power wheelchair to the mix on a first walk just didn't seem necessary when my new girl already had so much to adjust to. So it was "push power" courtesy of Dad to get us around the block.

As he, Maida, and I started off, she had no trouble adjusting to the pace of my wheelchair or keeping her paws clear of the wheels. Maida also was doing quite well at learning which side of my wheelchair she needed to walk on. Whereas dogs are usually taught to walk on a person's left side because that's the classic position for heeling, I needed Maida to walk on my right side because the controls for my power wheelchair were on the left. Even though Dad was at the controls for this walk, I knew it would be easier and faster for Maida to learn what I needed her to do when we were by ourselves if I asked her to walk on my right no matter which wheelchair I was using.

At the beginning, this walk was just like countless others I had been on with furry friends: smooth and uneventful. When we got to the end of our street and rounded the corner, though, things got interesting fast.

When assistance dogs are wearing their special harnesses, it's like a switch flips in them. Playtime is over. They are in working mode, and they know they need to be laser-focused on their human companions. All potential distractions disappear. Nothing matters except their job of helping their person whenever necessary.

When the harness comes off, the switch flips in the other direction. These specially trained dogs know they are off the clock and are free to act like "regular" dogs. For a Lab, that usually means eagerly greeting human or canine friends as quickly as possible when out and about. This eagerness rarely fades, whether it's the first meeting or the twenty-first. On Maida's first walk with me, she saw a Portuguese water dog from our neighborhood who also was out for a late afternoon walk with his dad. Maida and the neighbor dog had met on a previous walk and were already friends. She was no less eager to see her new buddy this time around.

As we came toward each other, I was in the process of switching Maida's leash from my left hand to my right. While in regular-dog mode, Maida had drifted over to my left side. I was trying to encourage her to move back to my right side but still had the leash mostly in my left hand. With my girl's new friend and her dad getting closer to us, Maida didn't care where she was supposed to be or where the leash was. As she bolted forward, the leash twisted around my left middle finger and bent it back until the leash pulled free. It happened so quickly that I didn't realize there was a serious problem at first. Maida probably wasn't away from my side for more than a minute or two. It was just long enough to say a quick hello, and then she came right back. Even so, I knew that if I tried to take the leash in my left hand again, I would be sorry.

When my mother and I went to the hospital later that evening, my injured finger had started to swell and turn purple around the second knuckle. An x-ray confirmed that in the battle of leash versus finger, my finger had clearly lost. I had a spiral fracture. That meant I had to spend six to eight weeks with my middle finger in a splint. Because I'm left-handed, that also meant I had to figure out new ways to do a lot of things—and that I needed more help than usual with some other everyday tasks—until my finger healed. Talk about a walk to remember.

It was probably at least eleven when Mom and I got home from the hospital that night. The stress of what had happened was finally catching up with me, not to mention the pain of my broken finger. I just wanted to change into my pajamas, get into bed, and get some much-needed shut-eye. But Maida had other ideas before I called it a night. As I was getting positioned on my back in bed, Maida walked into the room. Without waiting to be invited, she jumped up on my bed at the foot. I was still sleeping in a twin bed at the time, so there wasn't a lot of extra room for a sixty-five-pound dog. Maida didn't let a little thing like that stop her though. She walked up the length of my body, stopping when she reached my stomach. Then she looked directly in my eyes and bent down slightly so her forehead was touching mine. We stayed like that for several seconds. In that short time, I believe she was letting me know she loved me, she was sorry for what had happened, and she would never do anything like that again. From that night on, my girl was true to that unspoken message.

That interaction with Maida, though brief, had a profound impact on me. That was when I truly started to feel like she was becoming my dog. As Maida and I looked at each other, I hugged her, told her I loved her, and reassured her that everything would be OK. As I was talking to Maida, I could see out of the corner of one of my eyes that her tail was wagging. The pain in my finger was forgotten, and there are probably few other nights when I have slept as well.

Most people probably would consider my first walk with Maida a complete failure because of my broken finger. But I didn't then, and I don't now. Looking back on it, I know that twist of fate helped our relationship rather than hurt it. Instead of breaking our newly forming bond, the injury to my finger made that bond grow stronger even faster than it otherwise might have.

More than fifteen years after that fateful day of walking with Maida and decades after my first time holding Sandy's leash, walking with my dog remains a favorite activity. Since the pandemic began, taking a stroll around the neighborhood with my pup has become much more than my preferred way to spend at least an hour of free time on a day with good weather. When COVID-19 cases were at their highest where I live, walking with my current Lab, Rosie, became my main way to break free of my bubble and have any contact with the outside world. With so much uncertainty affecting nearly every aspect of life, I craved taking my dog for a walk because of the sense of normalcy and happiness it brought us both. In times where there is so much upheaval, an unexpected twist or turn would be the last thing I would want while doing a favorite activity. But on one particular walk in late winter 2021, Rosie showed me in her own way that an unexpected twist encountered while doing something that brings us great joy doesn't have to be a bad thing.

In the year and three months that I worked from home full-time, walking Rosie was the biggest highlight of every workday. As she got used to my teleworking routine, she seemed to know when quitting time was near. Every day as four thirty approached, she would walk into the dining room/office and look at me with a hopeful expression and wagging tail. *It's gotta be time*, she seemed to be saying. *Let's go*!

Sometimes I'd have to resist Rosie's considerable charms for at least a few minutes so I could finish an assignment. However, on that particular day, I was not willing to spend one extra second on work. It was March 11, 2021. The official start of spring was still about a week and a half away, but Mother Nature didn't care. She was ready to give us a preview. The sun was bright, temperatures were warm but a cool breeze was blowing, and the trees and flowers were showing off. Rosie and I didn't want to waste a second before taking advantage of the gorgeous late afternoon. After my mother helped me get into my power wheelchair and put Rosie's walking harness and leash on her, off my dog and I went.

Rosie must have enjoyed that first taste of spring as much as I did. When we got fairly close to the end of her preferred circuit around the neighborhood, she showed me that she wanted to extend her walk. We got to a curb cut that was a fork in the road on one of our other favorite routes, and Rosie pulled to indicate that she wanted to follow former New York Yankees catcher Yogi Berra's advice about that fork and take it. Seeing no harm, I agreed.

Things were fine until we passed a particular house where Rosie usually likes to sniff the bushes and flowers in the front yard. I call this reading the paper. Sniffing the surroundings on a walk is a dog's way of catching up on important neighborhood news like who else has come by, when, and most importantly what they may have left behind. With potentially hot stories close by but her nose just out of reach, Rosie moved from the right side of my power chair to the left. Like my other walking partners, Rosie learned early on why I need her to walk on the right side of my power wheelchair. However, Rosie occasionally pulls a switcheroo because she also knows that if she walks around to the opposite side of my chair and gets the leash twisted around the back, I will give her a treat when she pulls the leash free and gives it back to me. This walk threw us an unexpected twist though.

For the first time since I had walked one of my dogs in my power wheelchair, the leash got stuck somewhere when Rosie walked around to the left side. She tugged mightily to try to free it, but her efforts were to no avail. To further complicate this situation, no one was anywhere in sight to help us accomplish what Rosie could not. We were about halfway home at that point, but I could tell Rosie was a little unsure when we first resumed our walk because she knew she was on the other side of my chair instead of in her usual spot. I understood Rosie's uncertainty because I was more than a little worried myself. Even so, I knew I had to swallow that fear for her sake as well as my own. If I let Rosie see or hear that I was afraid, that could have made this mess even worse for both us.

When I realized Rosie was not in immediate danger and still had enough slack in the leash to walk comfortably beside me, we dealt with this latest twist of fate the only way I knew how. We kept moving forward. Her first few steps were a little hesitant, but as we started off, I stroked her head and back and talked to her in a calm and reassuring tone. Rosie hardly missed a beat after that—even when a pop-up rain-and-snow shower added another unexpected twist to the remainder of our walk. The main reason it took longer than usual to get home was that I was being extra careful to keep a slow pace. The last thing I wanted to do was bump my girl and potentially make her afraid to walk with me again. Another reason for our slower-than-usual roll was that I was looking to see if anyone might be outside who could untwist Rosie's leash from my wheelchair so we could get back on our usual track.

By this point dusk also was beginning to fall. Gathering darkness definitely can complicate things when you're trying to walk a dog while using a power wheelchair. Still, no one appeared to rescue Rosie and me from our predicament. With no helpers in sight, we just had to depend on each other. If Rosie slowed down, I slowed down. If she stopped, I did too. The streetlights were on by the time we finally arrived at our house, but we made it safely. When we got home, a neighbor who was outside freed Rosie from her tangled leash and took her into our house. He then alerted my mom to the situation, and they worked together to extract the twisted leash from my wheelchair.

Even though I was a little frightened at first when this latest twist of fate happened, I was quickly re-minded how lucky I was to have such a special dog by my side that day. Whenever Rosie looked at me during the rest of that walk after the twist occurred, her expression never showed fear. I could only see reassurance in her shining eyes and wide grin. She also never stopped giving me the ultimate form of encouragement a Labrador retriever can offer: a wag-ging tail! These simple signs of comfort may seem commonplace for a dog like Rosie, but they offered me some great insight about navigating life's twists and turns successfully. Even though it had a more dramatic outcome, my first walk with Maida several years earlier also taught me some equally valuable lessons about this topic.

Who we have beside us when the unexpected happens matters. Sometimes we see potential trouble coming; sometimes we don't. When something surprising crosses our path, it can cause our walking partner to veer off course temporarily. Sometimes this leads to difficult, even outright painful, consequences. If you find yourself in such a situation, try not to judge too harshly. Distractions and mistakes can happen to the best of us from time to time. What matters is how you handle them as they are happening and afterward. If you expect perfection from those who walk life's path with you, you will be sorely disappointed. Even though your loved ones may get offtrack once in a while, don't give up on them. Trust in the bond you have, and know that those who love you will return to your side and stay there to offer support rather than turning tail and continuing to run when things get challenging. Their calm, reassuring presence will bring out the best in you no matter how tricky a situation gets. Their faith in you will help you have renewed faith in yourself. It will show you that you are never truly alone.

Ultimately, your loved ones—regardless of their species—teach you that life's twists and turns don't have to leave you feeling helpless and tied up in knots. These setbacks don't have to break and scar you permanently either. Remarkably, they can do just the opposite. They can help you grow even stronger and closer together. They can help you see rainbows through the clouds.

Now You're Speaking My Language

Did you know the average dog knows about as many words as the average two-year-old? A 2009 study done by the American Psychological Association found that the average dog can understand about 165 spoken words, while dogs ranking in the top 20 percent of canine intelligence can learn the meaning of approximately 250 words. My guess is that just about any dog has been taught to understand words like *come*, *sit*, *stay*, *down*, *walk*, *potty*, *kibbles/supper*, and *treat*. Those words certainly seem essential for a dog to get through a day of living with us humans. I know they are in my house!

Dogs also typically know the names they associate with the people they live with. For example, in our pack my mother is "Mommy," my father is "Daddy," and I am "Girl." Every dog since Sandy has known us by these names. Other words in a dog's vocabulary come from places they visit often or activities they do regularly, in addition to words associated with basic obedience skills and tricks.

I am proud to say that several words in each of these categories have been part of our pack's collective canine vocabulary throughout the years. But our dogs also responded to some words that you might not expect. I already mentioned how our first Lab, Sandy, eventually understood that Saturday mornings in our house were always known as pancake day during her time with us. Dad also taught her to nudge our elbows with her nose when we stuck them out slightly from the edge of the kitchen table and spelled out n-u-z-z-l-e. That trick was always good for a treat, especially when Sandy thought the treats weren't coming fast enough.

Our golden retriever, Sable, was the first dog I can remember who responded to a request that was a mixture of verbal and nonverbal language. Like most golden retrievers, our Sable lived to love us, and we happily reciprocated. It took her very little time to learn that hugs were a sign of affection, not some kind of weird dominance ritual invented to make dogs submit to humans. When we opened our arms to her and asked for a hug, she quickly came to us and leaned in as far as she could, standing patiently the entire time as we wrapped our arms around her and stroked her. There was never a time when she misunderstood or ignored this request and the gesture that accompanied it. What's more, we could tell that our hugs meant as much to our dog as they did to us. If the hugger sat at her level, Sable frequently would rest her head on the person's shoulder during the embrace. What clearer sign could you ask for to show that the dog enjoyed this display of affection as much as the human did?

When it comes to extended vocabularies, our chocolate Lab, Snickers, knew one of the most unusual words of any dog in our pack. When dinnertime rolls around at our house, my dad is usually the one who fixes the dogs' food while Mom finishes getting the rest of the meal ready for us humans. Because Labs and golden retrievers have never been known for their patience when it's time to eat, they are usually done with their food before we have taken our first bite. As with most rules, though, there is often an exception. Snickers was ours in this case. For as long as I can remember, our family has had the tradition of praying before our evening meal. The prayer is usually a bit more involved around the holidays, but on every other night of the year, we gather around the table at dinnertime and say "God is great." When my sister and I said this prayer as children, we thought God was the only one who was listening. Until Snickers joined us, we had no idea that our dog might be paying attention to what we said before we ate.

For reasons we never understood, Snickers never stood to eat. After her bowl was filled, she would lie down with it between her paws and then wait a few moments before happily munching her kibbles. We often wondered what she was waiting for, so one night we decided to try to solve the mystery. Dad put the food in the dog's bowl as Mom was getting everything on the table for us. Then we sat down for our prayer. Everything was quiet as we said the blessing. After the *amen*, we waited for a few seconds to see what happened next. Our patience was rewarded with the sounds of Snickers starting to eat her own dinner! You might think this one instance was a fluke. But I tested it several other times when my parents went out to dinner with friends, leaving me and my pup home for the evening. The result was the same each time. Snickers always waited until I said the prayer and finished with *amen* before she and I both started to eat. She must have figured out that we said certain words before dinner and that it was important to wait until those words were done before we could enjoy the meal.

Snickers definitely was our biggest surprise when it came to understanding a spoken word. However, some of our other dogs also showed us it wasn't always necessary to use words to be understood. Maida was the first of our dogs to know sign language. She had already learned hand signals for many of her basic obedience cues, such as "sit," "stay," and "down," by the time she came to us. Seeing how successful Maida was with the sign language she knew, I also taught the same signs to Zeke when he was a pup. Along with these basic obedience hand signals, I taught both of my black Labs to touch my hand with their noses when I showed them the sign for "I love you."

Each of our dogs before our most recent girl, Rosie, had been a very skilled communicator in his or her own right. Not only did they respond appropriately to any of their verbal or nonverbal cues (most of the time!) but they also were quite adept at letting us know when they thought it was time for a meal, a potty break, or a walk. We could always count on them to tell us when someone was at the door too.

Of course, our dogs weren't doing the talking all the time. For as long as I can remember, all of us would say random things to our dogs throughout the day to amuse ourselves, ease our loneliness, or make ourselves feel better. We still do this now. On many days, it feels like I talk more to a dog than I do to the other people in the house. Can you relate? Regardless of the reason we talked to our earlier dogs, they always looked at us like we were the best, smartest people they had ever known. In every way that mattered, we understood one another. That said, I think our current girl and rescue pup, Rosie, may be our best canine communicator yet.

From her first days with us, Rosie has always been very in tune with and responsive to everyone in her pack. Like any Lab I have ever known, Rosie rejoices with us when we're happy and comforts us when we're sad. When it came to actual words, though, my parents and I had no idea how much of our language our new addition "spoke" or understood. The rescue worker who brought Rosie to us didn't know how much time, if any, someone had spent teaching her basic canine vocabulary. After she got used to being at home with us, I began to work with her on several essential cues—like "sit," "stay," "come," and "down"— at a training class. It wasn't very long before Rosie and I had mastered this basic language and were communicating very well at home and at school. However, it was several months before I saw how she would respond to me in a much less structured environment: that great adventure known as a walk.

Rosie came to us in October 2016, and we didn't go on our first walk together until July of the following year. My dad was Rosie's main walking companion during those first months because she pulled pretty hard while on her leash. My parents and I were afraid that without getting this behavior under control, she would pull away from me, and I wouldn't be able to get her back. After getting used to walking with someone and adjusting to a special harness to help with the pulling, Rosie set off with me for the first time. As we made our way down the driveway and out to the sidewalk, Rosie whined as if to say, *We can't go yet. We're forgetting Daddy.* I petted her and told her I would keep her safe. After I'd given her a treat as further proof that I would keep my promise, she looked over her shoulder at me and grinned. Her expression clearly showed what she was thinking at that moment. *Daddy who?* We were on our way.

Because this was our first walk and it was a hot day, I had planned to go a very short distance—just down to the end of our street and back, heading to the right out of our driveway. I knew that many walks with my father started in the same general direction, so I hoped this would give us the best chance for success on our first outing.

No matter how many times Rosie had walked in the same direction before, she was just as eager to investigate whatever interesting smells she caught wind of as if it were her first time passing by. As we started out, I was heartened by the fact that she likely was behaving the same way with me as she did with Dad. By the time we got to the second mailbox after our house, though, I wasn't quite so encouraged. Instead, I was genuinely afraid I would lose my dog, my right arm, or both because of how hard Rosie was pulling to sniff the latest intriguing scent she smelled. In my desperation to keep her from pulling away from me and to keep my arm attached to my body, I tried the only words I knew that might salvage the situation. I called out, "Rosie, wait!"

I initially became familiar with this cue when I had my assistance dog, Maida. I mainly used it when I wanted to get her through a door and then have her remain close by while I followed or when she pulled too far ahead of me on walks and I needed a moment or two to catch up. I had no idea whether Rosie understood this word or how she would respond. I just reacted because I knew it had worked before, and I was hoping with everything in me that it would work again.

Whether Rosie responded to the "wait" cue itself or to the slightly fearful edge that had crept into my voice, I will never know for sure. Maybe it was a combination of both. As soon as I asked her to wait, she stopped in her tracks and looked over her shoulder at me. The concern on her face was obvious. She didn't move a muscle until I caught up to her, patted her, and said, "Thank you so much, Rosie! Good girl! OK, go ahead." Had anyone else seen that incident, it might have looked like a lucky break. There probably was some luck involved, but I also saw it as a breakthrough moment. That was when I realized that Rosie and I truly were on our way to speaking to each other on a level that is much deeper than only understanding certain important words.

In the years since she has joined our pack, Rosie has shown that her ability to speak our language extends well beyond the basic vocabulary you might expect a dog to learn. Since she came to us, Rosie has shown that she understands when we need her help—no matter who is asking or what the job is. For example, Rosie learned her job of retrieving the Sunday paper in almost no time. All my dad has to do is look at her and say, "Rosie, it's Sunday. What do we do on Sunday?" Without fail, she pants excitedly and spins in front of him in gleeful anticipation of going outside to get the newspaper. Just a few minutes later, she trots through the back door with her prize in her mouth and her tail wagging proudly. When Dad tells her, "Take it to Mommy," she trots over to Mom and lets her take the paper—in exchange for some pets and a treat, of course.

Getting the paper every Sunday morning isn't the only job Rosie enjoys. She has shown the same eagerness to help by picking up things that I drop and giving them back to me. When she first learned the skill, I always had to use the verbal cue "take it" when I needed Rosie to retrieve something I had dropped. When she began to pick up dropped items, I also had to ask her to come to make sure she actually would bring them back to me. Both parts of this behavior are pretty much on autopilot now. Usually as soon as Rosie hears or sees something hit the floor, she is picking the item up and giving it to me before I've even asked for her help. She'll even do the same for my parents, usually without being asked.

Do you think it's just pure luck when members of two different species communicate without using words? If you do, here's a story that will change your mind. One day as I sat in my wheelchair in the family room watching a TV show while Rosie took a nap in front of the fireplace, she woke from her peaceful snooze at the sound of the remote hitting the carpet after I accidentally knocked it off the chair where it had been sitting. When Rosie heard the thump, she glanced at me, and I nodded. With just that subtle sign, she got up from her bed, walked over to the fallen remote control, picked it up, and gave it to me. She didn't even bump a button or get a drop of slobber on the controller in the process! I would have rewarded Rosie with one of her favorite treats immediately for such an outstanding retrieval, but at that moment, I didn't have anything tasty close by. Instead, I thanked her and showered her with kisses, pets, and scratches. Judging by the look on her face, that was worth more to her than an endless supply of Milk-Bones or whatever other treasure a dog might imagine seeing at the end of a rainbow.

I was—and still am—blown away by Rosie's ability to understand and respond appropriately in that moment without a word being spoken to her. This is even more remarkable because Rosie may not have had that much interaction with people before she came to us.

According to Rosie's rescue group, she had spent all but two weeks of her life tied to an outdoor dog box. The rescue worker who brought her to our house told us that the previous two weeks were the longest continuous stretch of time she had lived with people in their home. Perhaps understandably then, Rosie was a little shy around others at first. As her confidence has grown over time, so has her ability to relate to people of all ages she has never met before. Perhaps this is the most profound way Rosie can speak to people.

Take this example from a walk in early August 2021. When I returned home from the office that day, Rosie and I took our usual early evening stroll around the block. On this particular evening, something rather extraordinary happened.

As we were turning down the opposite side of our street to head for home, Rosie and I saw an older woman who was in her backyard enjoying some sunshine with a man who looked to be her son and a little boy whom I assumed was her grandchild. This woman had met Rosie a few times on previous walks, so she called out to my girl. When Rosie hears a greeting from a friend, she naturally wants to visit for a bit. When she heard this hello, she stopped, turned to look at the people, and whined as if to say, *Well, if you're gonna say hello, you have to come over and pet me*. After I explained this, they all got up from their lawn chairs and came to see us.

As the trio walked toward us, I noticed that the little boy looked very interested in Rosie. I greeted the child and asked if he'd like to pet her. At that point the woman explained that her grandson, who was just four years old at the time, was on the autism spectrum and was not very verbal. She quickly added that he really liked dogs. When they got to us, the child's grandmother told him that doggies liked to be scratched behind their ears. She followed that with a demonstration, which Rosie happily allowed. Seeing that the little boy still looked unsure of what he should do, I followed his grandmother's lead and encouraged him to give Rosie's ears a scratch. He did, much to my girl's delight. This progressed to some pats on Rosie's head and back.

After a few more minutes of pets for Rosie and chatting among the adults, the grandmother decided it was time for her and her family to go back home. She told her grandson to say goodbye to Rosie. She then put her own hand in the air, waved, and said, "Bye, Rosie!" Right after that, the boy waved his little hand in the air and said enthusiastically (and rather loudly), "Bye, Rodie!" The child's pronunciation of my dog's name wasn't perfect, but Rosie's shining eyes, cheerful grin, and wagging tail were clear proof that the slight mispronunciation didn't matter. She understood anyway. In fact, her reaction seemed to show more than just appreciation for her new friend's farewell. It was as if she recognized his accomplishment and wanted to celebrate with him.

As Rosie and I prepared to leave, the boy's grandmother shared that he had recently started attending a special school for children with disabilities. He was making strides in his language skills but wasn't yet saying much around other people—especially people he didn't know. This made the fact that he had never met me before but still had said Rosie's name during their first meeting a very big deal.

As I absorbed what I had just learned, I had to believe that something in Rosie spoke to this little boy and encouraged him to respond to her in a way he couldn't do with too many people yet. This brief encounter offered some powerful lessons. It matters who walks beside you throughout your life's journey, so choose your companions wisely. Surround yourself with friends and loved ones who not only can comfort you when rain and clouds appear but also will wait with you and celebrate joyfully when the rainbow comes. Look for others who listen to understand and to be understood, sometimes without speaking a word. Your nearest and dearest should recognize and celebrate every achievement, large or small. They also should notice and appreciate the special gifts that are unique to you—no matter how each of you expresses yourself. Perhaps most important of all, seek to be closest to those who can look past differences on the surface and see how you are similar in the ways that matter most. Doing this will help bring out the best in everyone and encourage you to see the best in one another. Do you agree with what I'm talking about? Now you're speaking my language!

PART 3

A Rainbow Comes Shining Through

God puts rainbows in the clouds so that each of us—in the dreariest and most dreaded moments—can see a possibility of hope.

—Maya Angelou, African American
author and poet

You'll never find a rainbow if you're looking down.

—Charlie Chaplin, English comic actor,
filmmaker, and composer

Be thou the rainbow in the storms of life.
The evening beam that smiles the clouds away,
And tints tomorrow with prophetic ray.

—Lord Byron, English Romantic poet

Rainbow Connections

After sharing so many personal stories, I'd like to pause for some self-reflection. If the title of this story makes you think of Jim Henson's lovable Muppets characters in their movie debut, you likely have plenty of company. Close your eyes and let your mind wander back to the opening scenes of *The Muppet Movie*. You can see Kermit the Frog sitting on a log in his swamp. You can hear him strumming his banjo and singing about the magic, wonder, and spellbinding beauty of rainbows. Kermit acknowledges that we've been told that "rainbows are visions, but only illusions"—nothing more than tricks our eyes play on us. But in his heart, Kermit knows these doubters are wrong. He knows that if he keeps his faith, believes in himself, and follows his dreams, he'll find what he's looking for in life.

Even with his eternal optimism, I think Kermit realizes it won't be easy for any of us to create the life we want. He seems to understand that sometimes clouds will move in front of the rainbow we're following. But if we truly believe in our dreams and want to make them come true, we won't lose sight of them for long. We'll keep our heads up and our eyes open. We'll wait until the clouds break and we can see our rainbow in front of us once more. We'll keep moving toward the treasure we believe awaits us at our rainbow's end.

As he looks skyward while singing, Kermit asks, "What's so amazing that keeps us stargazing, and what do we think we might see?" I don't think everyone's favorite frog expects an answer to such a profound question right away. I also think he knows that the answers will be different for everyone who's brave enough to ask such a deep question. But Kermit believes each of us will find the answer we're looking for if we stay hopeful and keep searching. "Someday we'll find it," he sings. "The rainbow connection. The lovers, the dreamers, and me."

This classic song from a well-loved family movie shows how rainbows speak to us and connect us on a simple but profound level. For one thing, I don't know anyone who isn't happy to see a rainbow. But rainbows offer more than just momentary natural beauty. In many cultures around the world, they represent hope, good luck, new beginnings, peace, connection to loved ones, spiritual guidance, and the promise of better days to come. Who among us couldn't use more of at least some of these blessings at some point in our lives? I'll be the last to refuse should any of those gifts come my way.

Have you ever noticed that rainbows, whether natural or symbolic, usually appear after clouds and rain have come? When rainbows do come, they usually don't last very long either—unlike the struggle, sadness, or disappointment we went through to get to see the rainbow in the first place.

Rainbows frequently inspire many good feelings in the people who see them. But in the busyness and stress of everyday life, feelings such as hope and peace and the promise of a fresh start can be just as fleeting as the source of their inspiration. Don't we wish we could hold on to such positive feelings when we have them? No one I know wants to feel bad all the time. Who would enjoy going through life feeling as if there's no relief from the dark clouds and rain? I also don't know anyone who actually looks forward to experiencing something bad before the good comes. Can't we just get right to the good parts of life sometimes, and can't we savor them so they last long after the experience ends?

Unlike Kermit the Frog in *The Muppet Movie*, most of us probably haven't decided to leave our homes and travel across the country to follow our dreams of Hollywood stardom. Although if you are brave enough to chase that kind of rainbow, I wish you much luck. I think what a lot of people—myself included—truly want is to find a way to see the best in every day and make the best out of every day, no matter where we are and what our circumstances may be. We don't necessarily want to wait until conditions are just right to find what we're looking for either. We want to learn to see something extra in the ordinary to lighten our days. Then we can hold on to that light and move toward it if times are cloudy or rainy—or even if they aren't. We can see rainbows anywhere and anytime. What's more, we can share the light with others who may need help finding their own way.

I hope this final group of stories will help you see that you don't have to wait for a rainy day or season to increase your chances of seeing a rainbow. You can see one throughout the year whenever you need it, and it may appear in an unusual place when you least expect it. Just keep your head up, look for the light, and share what you find so everyone can spread it. This way we can work together to chase the clouds away and make everything shine a little brighter.

You Say You Want a Resolution?

How do you ring in the New Year? Maybe your celebration includes going to a New Year's Eve party, either in person or virtually. Maybe you go to dinner and a movie with a few close friends or family members. Maybe you watch New Year's Eve celebrations from around the country on TV. Or maybe you just take your old calendar off the wall, flip to the first page of a new one, and keep going with your life as usual.

For the past few years, I haven't spent the last night of December counting down the final ten seconds until midnight while waiting for a ball to drop in Times Square and anticipating a kiss from the special man in my life. Instead, I have watched a college football game or two after dinner and then gone to bed with a couple of hours of the outgoing year to spare. As for New Year's Day, our family's celebration involves getting together for a full slate of college football games and a dinner of pork, sauerkraut (for most of us), mashed potatoes, peas, and applesauce, with a leftover Christmas cookie for dessert if we have room.

No matter how you choose to mark the start of another year, perhaps you are among the many people who make at least one resolution when the calendar changes from December 31 to January 1. Most of us pledge to do things like eat a healthier diet, exercise more, or lose weight. Saving more while spending less is also a popular goal. Even though we have good intentions to make the most of the fresh start a new year offers, many of us don't stick to our goals for more than a couple of weeks. Maybe some of us can hang on for a few months if we're really motivated. I wouldn't know about that. Among people who made at least one resolution in 2020, slightly more than one-third kept them all, about half kept some, and everyone else failed at keeping any resolutions.

Each of the goals I mentioned has made my list of resolutions for every New Year's Day in recent memory. Others I have aspired to achieve include going to church more often, striving to be better organized, and being less inclined to put off difficult tasks. Like so many other people, I start the first day of January with the best of intentions: this will finally be the year I stick to my resolutions. However, my resolve wanes after a few weeks, and I end up back in the same old patterns I was so sure I would finally break. If you find yourself stuck in the same cycle at the start of every year, maybe what we need is a resolution revolution.

I was introduced to a similar idea a few years ago by a man named Father Bill Miller, who is a friend of my mother's brother and his wife. Father Bill is now an Episcopal priest in Texas; he also has written three books. My aunt and uncle first met Father Bill when he was a priest on the island of Kauai, Hawaii. He served at the church they attend when they vacation there. My aunt and uncle first introduced me and my family to Father Bill's writings, including his blog, about seven years ago. One of his blog posts in early 2015 encouraged me to take a broader look at New Year's resolutions. His ideas have stuck with me ever since, and I'd like to share them with you here in my own words.

Rather than traditional resolutions, Father Bill believes we should focus on New Year's restitutions, absolutions, and evolutions. None of us is God, so there is no doubt that we all have made plenty of mistakes throughout any given year. What's done is done. We can't go back and change the past, but we can acknowledge when we have done something wrong and do our best to make restitution. In other words we can do everything in our power to make the wrong right. This is important not only in the moment but also as part of a heartfelt attempt to make sure we don't repeat the same mistake in the future.

We all have had days where nothing seems to go right no matter how hard we try. Sometimes those days stretch into weeks, months, or possibly even years. We may not feel as if we have any reason to be grateful or any hope that our situation will improve. But no matter how bleak our outlook, no matter how dark the storm clouds seem, there is always room for a ray of light. I think it's this: sometimes the biggest thing we can be grateful for at the end of the day is the chance to learn from our mistakes and try to make tomorrow better.

Along with the opportunity to right past wrongs comes the chance to offer forgiveness—to absolve ourselves and each other of past mistakes and to wipe the slate clean. So often we are taught to forgive others for the hurt they have caused us and to not hold grudges. Father Bill stresses that it's just as important to forgive ourselves for our own short-comings. We can never truly improve our lives if we are stuck in a pattern of beating up on each other or ourselves. If we only focus on everything that has gone wrong, we'll become trapped in a vicious, never-ending cycle of finger-pointing and blame. We'll miss seeing all the positive things in our lives, along with any opportunities to make what is wrong right.

Along with New Year's restitutions and absolutions, we have evolutions. Growth can happen as a result of all types of experiences. Growing pains aren't just for socially awkward teenagers. We all have them at various stages of life. Growing pains are hard, and they hurt no matter when they hit, but they will ultimately help if these challenges help us grow into better, stronger people.

Your New Year's resolution might be something concrete, like losing fifty pounds before the end of the year, saving twenty dollars out of every paycheck, or exercising three times a week. Mine might be something more abstract, like working to be less judgmental and more forgiving of myself and others. All are worthy goals. Regardless of whether your resolution focuses on something physical, mental, or spiritual, it seems to me that lasting change can't happen without first getting our minds and hearts in the right places to make the change. When that happens, the rest should fall into place.

Changes this big won't happen overnight. They also may not happen without some kind of inspiration. To guide me in my efforts for future New Year's resolutions, I plan to focus on three fortunes from past Chinese take-out meals. I've pinned the little papers to my cubicle wall at work. Each one is several years old, but all of them still ring true today—so much so that I even made sure they survived a move to a different office building.

If you care enough for a result, you will most certainly attain it. Hard work that you put your mind and heart into leads to good results. The payoff may not be instant, but if you truly care about something, you'll be willing to put forth the effort necessary to achieve your goal. What's more, you'll appreciate what you have that much more because of how hard you worked to get it. The rainbow will be much more meaningful because you persevered through the rain.

Give to the world the best you have, and the best will come back to you. This seems clear enough. Put good out, and you'll get back so much more than you imagined. If you share light that you have with others, it cannot help but reflect. This will make things brighter for everyone around you, as well as for yourself.

Be a first-rate version of yourself rather than a second-rate version of someone else. You may have heard the saying "Imitation is the sincerest form of flattery." This means that the highest compliment you can give other people is to be like them. That sounds great at first. However, it's only true if you've chosen a good role model. Another possible issue with imitating someone else? It's often easy to spot a fake a mile or more away. Life is hard enough without trying to be someone you aren't. No one else can be you quite the same way you can. That said, there is nothing wrong with trying to incorporate lessons you learn or traits you admire in other people into your own life. But don't try to *be* the other person. Each of us is truly a designer original. Why not concentrate your efforts on being the absolute best *you* that you can be rather than trying to copy someone else?

I WILL NEVER ARGUE THAT RESTITUTION, absolution, and evolution don't have their places in making lives better day after day, year in and year out. You say you want a resolution? I think we need one more tool in our toolboxes to start the first day of every year—and every day thereafter—on the right foot. As I see it, we need to undergo a resolution revolution. We need to work on changing our mindset from one of tearing down to one of building up, to one of working toward solutions instead of becoming mired in our problems. Said another way, we need to find and share the rainbows instead of focusing on the rain.

Happiness Is...

I suspect it would be very hard to be happy all the time. But life's struggles and disappointments sure would be easier to manage if we looked for rainbows instead of worrying about rain clouds.

I generally agree with the theory that money can't buy happiness, except on one point. A few years ago, I had a Page-A-Day calendar that offered a daily dose of wisdom, insight, or even a little humor to help get through the day. These little nuggets usually centered on a common theme. The year I had this calendar, that theme was "Keep calm and carry on." Each day featured a quote that spoke to the importance of staying calm and happy and continuing to move forward no matter what challenges we face.

One source of inspiration for this story came from the daily quote for February 17. As fate would have it, that's not far from the day on which my family and friends most often wish me happiness: my birthday. On February 17 American writer Gene Hill offered the following reminder about happiness: "Whoever said money can't buy happiness forgot about puppies." Hear, hear! Many of the happiest, most enduring memories of my life involve at least one of my pups. These memories were not all made in my dogs' younger days either. I think my family would agree that the money we have spent (and are still spending) to have at least one dog as part of our pack has been one of the best long-term happiness investments we ever made. On the day that I am no longer sharing my life with a dog, I will feel quite poor indeed. Nothing I could buy would ever fill that void.

As it turns out, Gene Hill isn't the only person who thinks dogs are key to our happiness. Charles Schulz does too. Many people know this American cartoonist as the creator of the popular comic strip *Peanuts*, which debuted in 1950. This comic strip may be Charles Schulz's biggest claim to fame; however, he also wrote hundreds of books featuring his beloved characters. My favorite among these is the other big source of inspiration for this story. It seems to me that Charles Schulz's philosophy about dogs and the joy they bring to people's lives can be summed up in five words: *Happiness Is a Warm Puppy*. You may recognize this as the title of his first book, which was originally published in 1962. It encourages readers to find happiness in the simple pleasures of everyday life. Whether you believe this book is strictly for kids or for the kid in each of us, I want to use it, along with two of my favorite *Peanuts* TV specials, as inspiration for what I think happiness means to three of my favorite characters—and why I think the wisdom Charles Schulz shares still matters.

Let's look at Charlie Brown first. You may find it ironic that a valuable lesson about happiness comes from a boy who often seems just a little bit sad. Consider this example from my favorite holiday TV special, *A Charlie Brown Christmas*. Early in the story, Charlie says he feels depressed because he's struggling to understand the true meaning of Christmas. In an effort to lift his spirits, Lucy says he should direct their Christmas play. Beaming from ear to ear about the idea, Charlie Brown heads to the school auditorium with the others to get started on the project.

If you've seen this special, you know it's not long before Lucy takes over as director and assigns Charlie Brown the task of getting a tree to help with creating the right atmosphere for the play. All the kids tell him to bring back the biggest, shiniest tree he can find. When Charlie and Linus get to the tree lot, they find themselves surrounded by a forest of metal trees. In the midst of all that artificiality, Charlie and Linus spot the lone real tree. Despite its scrawny, scraggly appearance—or maybe because of it—Charlie is drawn to the little tree. He chooses it because he thinks it needs him. As you probably know, Charlie Brown is laughed out of the auditorium for bringing back exactly the type of tree that the other kids didn't want. But he doesn't let that discourage him or dampen the Christmas spirit he's starting to feel. Charlie takes the little tree home and decorates it. By the end of the show, all the other kids end up loving the tree they had laughed at before. All smiles, they gather around it to sing a Christmas carol and wish Charlie Brown a merry Christmas.

This classic show offers a powerful lesson about happiness. You don't always have to follow the crowd to find it. Sometimes situations can turn out even better than expected if you follow your own heart in the search for happiness instead.

Next, let's consider what happiness is to Linus. If you ever read the *Peanuts* comic strip or watched any of the TV specials, you know Lucy's little brother is never without his blanket. Maybe you can relate to something similar from your own childhood.

When you're young, the simplest things can give you the courage you need to overcome your fears and feel safer and more confident. The older you get, the more sophisticated your security blankets likely will become. However, no matter how old you get or how strong you may think you are, you don't have to prove your bravery by facing down whatever frightens you alone. We all have times when we need a little extra help to feel safe and secure. Looking for that help isn't showing a sign of weakness or giving in to fear. Getting help to fight fear shows it that you won't just give up and let it win. Why not think about how you might provide that sense of safety, bravery, confidence, and comfort to someone in need?

Many people might only picture Linus with his blanket if they think about what happiness means to him. I don't disagree with that image. However, my mind also goes to another place when I picture happiness for Linus. I have no problem imagining him running toward a leaf pile and jumping in.

For my own proof of the happiness a freshly raked mound of leaves can bring, I need look no further than my dog Zeke. No other dog my family has known and loved appreciated a good leaf pile as much as he did. One of my favorite pictures of him as a puppy was taken when he was probably five or six months old. It shows Zeke sitting chest deep in a pile of leaves and looking intently at the camera. He was apparently completely unaware that another leaf was positioned perfectly on top of his head. Similarly, there is another photo where he is almost completely submerged in a leaf pile with only his head above the surface. Those were just two of many such photos taken throughout his life.

My family and I don't know what attracted Zeke to leaf piles. Maybe at first, it was the rustling sound they made as he walked through them. Maybe the texture of the leaves somehow appealed to him. As he got older, I think he continued to lie in the leaf piles because he knew how much we enjoyed seeing him do it. Every fall from his first to his last, I took pictures of Zeke in the leaves the way some people take pictures of their children on the first day of school. The difference was that I could never stop with just one or two. I needed more like ten or twenty.

To bring this anecdote back to the beloved characters who helped inspire it, I recall one of my favorite scenes in the classic Halloween TV special *It's the Great Pumpkin, Charlie Brown*. Charlie has just finished raking all the leaves into a huge pile. As soon as this chore is done, his friend Linus comes charging straight toward the pile and takes a flying leap right into it. We can hear Charlie exclaim, "Good grief!" before the words are even out of his mouth. As a child, I could completely understand Charlie Brown's frustration. He had just finished a hard job, and then along came his friend to undo everything he had just done. Some friend. When I see this familiar scene as an adult, my reaction is completely different. I inwardly cheer for Linus now. In fact, if I could somehow witness this scene in person today, I would take pictures to capture the moment. I would even run alongside Linus and jump in the pile with him if I could. Sometimes just like Charlie Brown did, we need a friend to show us how to let go of our frustration. Forget about raking the leaves again. Forget about finally kicking the football this year. Instead, dive straight into something you know is within reach and give yourself permission to truly enjoy the moment.

Finally, let's think about what happiness is to Lucy. Are you completely stumped? Do you think her only happiness comes from putting other kids down? I can understand why you would think that. But here's an idea that could change your way of thinking. Every timeless tidbit of wisdom shared in *Happiness Is a Warm Puppy* comes with its own drawing by Charles Schulz to illustrate the point. It may surprise you to know that the accompanying illustration for this title truism does not feature Charlie Brown and his best pal sharing a hug. Instead, it shows Lucy hugging Snoopy. In the cartoons and comic strips, Lucy always complained about the poisonous germs she surely had contracted from her lips touching dog lips. If Lucy can eventually accept Snoopy's love, I think there's hope that even the most reluctant among us can find happiness from an unexpected source if we're open to the possibility.

Each of these examples of happiness from Charles Schulz is great. No doubt there are countless other pieces of advice each of us could add to our own personal happiness lists. Maybe the greatest source of happiness is something that isn't mentioned in Charles Schulz's little book or in the TV shows that feature his characters. Happiness is knowing that we have people who love us who will share in whatever life brings our way. They will encourage us when we stumble. They will cheer with us and for us when we succeed. Perhaps most important of all, when clouds come our way, as they inevitably will, these people will stay with us while it rains. When the storm ends, they will help us look for the rainbow. By doing that they can teach us to be a rainbow for someone else.

Blooming Where You Are Planted

My parents and I have lived in the same home for more than three decades. Every year except our first, my mother has kept beautiful planting beds in front of the house. Among other varieties of flowers, she has had daffodils, crocuses, hyacinths, tulips, and pansies. Every spring the front yard would blossom in a joyous riot of colors: pink, purple, yellow, white, and maybe even a splash of red here and there. Seeing the leaves push through the cold, hard earth was a sure sign that warmer weather would be here soon. When the flowers finally opened, you couldn't help but smile. Spring had finally sprung!

While the flowers always brought my mother and me a lot of happiness, they had the opposite effect on my father. This never failed to perplex us. Aside from laying the mulch to prepare for planting, Dad rarely participated in the day-to-day care of Mom's flower beds. If anything, his efforts to help usually resulted in Mom getting upset because Dad often would mistake a perfectly healthy flower for a weed and uproot it.

At the time, my father was approaching retirement after more than forty years as a dentist in private practice. Many people I know look at their upcoming retirement as a chance to rediscover or reinvent themselves—an opportunity to figure out who they are apart from the job that defined their lives for so many years. People often explore new hobbies as they look for ways to spend some of their newfound free time.

Before my father started to anticipate the next chapter of his life, he became laser-focused on removing current sources of stress. He must have decided that Mom's flower beds were a major source of stress for him—probably because of the mulching and weeding associated with making the planting beds so lovely. In the year leading up to his retirement, my dad conspired with a landscaper to overhaul the look of my mother's planting beds by replacing the mulch with a weed barrier and brown stones. Clearly, then, Dad had never envisioned gardening in his postretirement days.

My mother and I were dismayed when we found out that Dad and his coconspirator were plowing ahead with this plan. Mom didn't get a vote on it, and her name is on the deed to the house. I knew there was no way my opinion would matter, but this certainly didn't seem like an "improvement" to me.

What would happen to our beautiful flowers, which had always been a first sign of happier, brighter, more hopeful days to come? Would they be able to break through the weed barrier and the stones and bloom as they had before?

The first day of spring came and went that year, and my sense of anticipation was dashed. Nothing. Not even the slightest bit of green was peeking through our "new and improved" flower beds. For the first time ever, I was a little envious and sad when I took my dog for a walk that day and saw flowers popping up in other yards in the neighborhood. But several weeks later...victory! Daffodils, a few crocuses, and even an iris appeared among the stones that had taken over Mom's flower beds. Then the hostas, which were my mother's most recent planting experiment, began their comeback. What made each flower's reappearance in its new environment even more impressive was that it happened without any TLC from Mom. Despite Dad's apparent intent to simplify and de-stress his life (and add stress to ours!) by making over the flower beds, the sunlight and rain must have been able to penetrate through the stones just enough to allow some flowers to push through the weed barrier when the time was right.

When change happens in life, it's often said that we don't truly appreciate what we had until it's gone. That's not just true for the one who got away. It also can be true for anything that brought us happiness, comfort, or satisfaction in life. If something we once enjoyed or looked forward to is suddenly no longer part of our daily routine, life may lack a little of the luster it had before. That's why when we experience an unexpected comeback, we tend to appreciate what we have even more and take better care of it the second time around. This is true whether we are talking about something as simple as a flower blooming in a less-than-hospitable environment or something as complex as mending a relationship with a friend or a loved one.

As I have watched some of my mother's flowers continue to bloom each year in their refurbished home, I realize that such "flower power" can teach us a lot about ourselves. Everyone's "rock bottom" is different. It may come in the form of a broken relationship that we expected to last a lifetime or a sudden illness. It could be the loss of a lifelong job that forces us to reexamine our identity and purpose in life. It could be an addiction to drugs, alcohol, or gambling that consumes us so quickly that, before we know it, we have lost everything we once held so dear.

I have heard that the only way a person can truly know rock bottom is to hit it. I sincerely hope that never happens to you. But if it does, remember that the only way to go from there is up. I hope the story of my mother's flowers is one example of how rock bottom does not have to mean the end of something that was once beautiful, strong, and vibrant. Even in the bleakest of circumstances, goodness, beauty, strength, hope, and resilience still can flourish. For this to happen, your roots must be deep enough and strong enough to withstand whatever change comes. Then you must take the showers and the sunshine as they appear, using each to help you not only grow and survive but also bloom season after season. Just as rainbows need both showers and sunshine to come to life, people do too.

Maybe the biggest lesson flowers can teach is this: we cannot always control where we are planted, but no matter our surroundings, we can choose whether to bloom or to wither. My choice—and yours too, I hope—would be to bloom and, ultimately, to thrive.

Eating the Elephant
in the Room

If you've read some of my earlier stories, you know how important and special dogs have always been to me. You might even think they're the only animal I like. But there is some room in my heart for others. If I had to choose a favorite wild animal, it definitely would be the elephant. Like a lot of people, I was first exposed to elephants during visits to the circus as a child. Watching elephants under the big top, I remember being in awe of their size, as well as how gentle they seemed. I would have loved to be a performer who worked with one of the massive creatures—hanging on to its harness as I rode around the center ring, doing all sorts of acrobatic tricks on its back, and being caught by its long trunk as our finale. The elephants also seemed so friendly as they stood in a line on their hind legs with their front legs up on one another's backs and their trunks raised high as if they were waving to the crowd when the act was over. What kid couldn't love that?

My fascination with elephants continued throughout my childhood when we would take day trips to the zoo when visiting my grandparents in South Carolina. I could have sat in front of that enclosure for hours watching the elephants eat, bathe, or just bask in the sun. Of course, that childlike enjoyment came rushing back when I saw elephants during a trip to the Animal Kingdom at Disney World, even though I had been an adult for many years by that time.

Elephants became more than an exotic circus or zoo animal to me several years ago after I saw a "Making a Difference" segment on *NBC Nightly News*. The segment focused on a nonprofit organization called the Sheldrick Wildlife Trust. This is a group that rescues and rehabilitates injured or orphaned African elephants and rhinoceroses. Their website also has an adoption program where you can donate to assist with the animals' care. As you might expect, the elephants who are helped by this program have not had the best start in life. Many of them are quite young—no more than two or three years old at most. The youngest elephants to benefit from this program, I learned while watching the news report, were orphaned shortly after birth as the mothers were victims of poaching. By this point in the segment, I had already decided I would make at least one donation to the cause. Maybe I would contribute regularly. But the impact of this news report didn't stop there.

It actually did something I never thought would be possible: it made me envious of Chelsea Clinton. She was the special guest, which meant she got to visit the sanctuary and meet some of the elephants. She even fed one of the babies from a bottle. If only...

Not only did this report touch my heart but it also inspired me to learn more about elephants. Some of the things I learned? Elephants live in fairly large groups with a complex social structure that is similar to human families. In fact, some people may argue that elephant families are superior to their human counterparts. In elephant society the women are in charge. But I digress. Elephants are similar to humans in other ways too. Pachyderms are highly intelligent and have excellent memories. Like humans, elephants can feel a wide range of emotions. Researchers have documented plenty of examples of elephants displaying joy, whether in the wild or in captivity. As you might expect, this commonly happens during such events as the birth of a new calf or a reunion with a family member or friend. On the opposite end of the emotional spectrum, elephants can experience extreme sadness, given that they mourn following the loss of a family member or friend, much like humans do.

Perhaps because of their commonalities with humans, elephants are revered in many cultures. In China, India, and Africa, they symbolize power, strength, dignity, intelligence, wisdom, and peace.

Elephants also symbolize "higher power" qualities such as divinity and benevolence. In many Asian cultures, an elephant with its trunk raised is a sure sign of good fortune.

Given the magnificence of these creatures and all the wonderful qualities they represent, you can imagine my surprise when a family friend and former neighbor once asked me, "How do you eat an elephant?"

My initial thought was, *I think elephants are great. Besides, they're endangered. Why would I ever want to eat one?* But I sensed a larger, more insightful point to this question. This man's questions and stories always had great points, and I was curious to see where this one would go. I thought a minute or two and gave him the best response that came to mind. "I don't know," I said. "The same way you eat anything, I guess—with a knife and fork and maybe a spoon."

I should have known there was a deeper answer to this inquiry. It was so riddlelike that the response couldn't have been straightforward. It turned out I was right. The answer my former neighbor had in mind was much more metaphorical. Here it is: "You eat an elephant one bite at a time. It doesn't matter where you start as long as you finish the whole thing."

Huh. Why couldn't I think of that?

Our family's friend posed this question to me in the midst of particularly difficult circumstances I was facing at my first job after college. I haven't talked much about this to anyone outside my family, except a close friend or two. Though it has been more than fifteen years since this incident happened, I'm not going to break my silence here. Suffice it to say, it had to do with my disability.

You have probably heard of the elephant in the room—that difficult situation that's beyond uncomfortable to talk about but that looms so large it cannot be ignored no matter how hard you try. The only way to get these elephants out of our rooms so we can get on with life is to eat them bite by bite. These elephants we eat may take many forms. They could be unexpected health issues, strained relationships, problems at work, financial challenges, or any number of other things that give us a good old-fashioned gut check. As with even the hardest situations you face, there's some good news here. You may have to eat the elephant (or at least most of it), and you can only handle manageable bites. But it doesn't matter which part of the elephant you eat first as long as you finish. Our family's friend also never said you couldn't have anyone else in the room with you for encouragement or support. Maybe that trusted friend or loved one could pick up a knife and fork—or maybe a spoon—and eat a bite or two of the elephant with you.

Reflecting on that chat years later, I see how correct my neighbor was. Our conversation is the reason I keep a small marble elephant figurine—with its trunk raised—in plain sight on my desk at work. In the years since that conversation, I also have come to understand that these elephants we eat need not always be the scary kind that we fear will trample us to death. Life events such as going off to college, starting a new job, moving out on your own, getting married, or having a child can seem like elephantine challenges when you are just contemplating them—much less when you are in their midst. But with courage, time, patience, and help, you can work through them and realize that what you may have been terrified to even think about actually turned out to be very rewarding. Maybe it was one of the best decisions you ever made.

This elephant analogy brings to mind another old saying that I think has relevance here: "You are what you eat." If we eat whatever elephant is on our plate one bite at a time, at the very least when we're through, we'll have a pretty tough hide. This, I might add, can only enable us to take on more and bigger challenges as time goes on. But here's a reminder of what else we'll gain when we eat these elephants: power, strength, dignity, intelligence, wisdom, and peace. We also can't forget about benevolence and a healthy shot of good fortune. When all of these qualities combine, that actually sounds like a pretty tasty meal, doesn't it?

So the next time an elephant of some sort crosses your path, take a deep breath while you decide whether you should run in the opposite direction or stay where you are. Resist the urge to feel over-whelmed or intimidated by the elephant, and don't try to avoid it. Pick up your knife and fork—and maybe a spoon—and start eating one bite at a time. Chew each bite slowly and carefully so you can absorb all that each morsel has to offer. And no matter what, keep your trunk up.

Discovering Your Superpower

When I wrote about superheroes in my blog, the inspiration for that entry was not what you'd probably expect. Since I was a child in the 1980s, you might think that characters like Superman, He-Man, She-Ra, Wonder Woman, or countless others got my creative juices flowing. It's true that I spent many hours watching their exploits on Saturday mornings or as an after-school treat, but they weren't the ones who sparked my imagination about this topic so many years later. As an adult I realize that not all superheroes wear capes. What's more, not all superheroes look like people. Given what I've shared about myself, it may not be too surprising to know that the original inspiration for my blog entry was dogs—specifically dogs specially trained to assist people with disabilities.

International Assistance Dog Week is observed each year, starting on the first Sunday in August. It began in 2011 as a way to celebrate the impact that assistance dogs make in the lives of their human partners. It also recognizes the commitment, compassion, and dedication of people who are willing to raise, train, and foster these very special dogs. I was fortunate beyond measure that my beautiful and whip-smart black Lab Maida—who had originally been partnered with a man who had rheumatoid arthritis—eventually found her way to me and my family. Her superpowers, including the ability to retrieve dropped items and open doors, were a great help to me in overcoming some of my physical challenges. Despite my good fortune in having a fully trained assistance dog for eight years, I was not aware of International Assistance Dog Week until a few years ago at work when I attended a web-based seminar about assistance dogs as a workplace accommodation for people with disabilities.

The accompanying PowerPoint handout for this seminar featured photos of several assistance dogs in various work settings helping their human partners. This simple visual aid conveyed a powerful message. Having a disability doesn't have to be a roadblock or a hindrance to the life you want to lead. Living with a disability can be just another day at the office—especially when you have a capable canine companion standing by to help when needed.

In the past, people's primary image of an assistance dog's role was probably to guide people with visual impairments. But assistance dogs today can be trained to provide help in many other ways. Besides retrieving dropped objects and opening doors, dogs also can help people with mobility impairments by providing balance so their owners can safely stand or transfer to or from their wheelchairs. Some dogs are strong enough to pull wheelchairs. Dogs can be superheroes for people with hearing impairments by alerting them to ringing phones, knocks at the door, or beeping smoke alarms. Assistance dogs working today also can be trained to detect seizures and changes in blood sugar, which makes them life-savers for people with conditions such as epilepsy and diabetes. Last but certainly not least, people dealing with posttraumatic stress disorder, anxiety disorders, and similar conditions can be helped tre-mendously by the calming, reassuring presence of an assistance dog. Their list of superpowers really does seem endless!

This presentation contained one slide that fea-tured an assistance dog in a special vest standing at attention. It was as if the dog's expression said, *Here I am! What can I do to help? I've got you.*

The text that accompanied the slide was written as if the dog were speaking. In a nutshell it said that the dog could do things like lower blood pressure, reduce the levels of hormones that trigger the hu-man body's "fight or flight" responses, and increase chemicals that contribute to feelings of love and trust. This slide also pointed out that assistance dogs can make social interactions between their human partners and other people easier, thus reducing ste-reotypes, stigmas, and other social barriers associ-ated with disabilities. Assistance dogs also can help boost their partners' productivity and increase their independence. All those powers sound quite super to me.

At the bottom of this slide, the assistance dog posed this question to the audience: What's your superpower? Whether a dog's superpowers come as a result of intensive, specialized training or just by a lucky roll of the genetic dice, this simple but powerful question made me think. If a dog can do all this to help other people, what can I do if I work hard and really make an effort to try to help however I can? What *is* my superpower?

As a child I might have wished for things like superhuman strength, x-ray vision, the ability to fly, invisibility, time travel, or the ability to heal sick or injured people or animals. When none of those materialized no matter how hard I wished, it prob-ably didn't take me long to forget about them. But thoughts of superpowers can return easily when you are an auntie to two children as imaginative as my niece and nephew are.

My nephew first showed an interest in super-heroes when he was four. He and one of his bud-dies from school talked quite a lot about someone named Ultimate Man. When my nephew decided that's who he wanted to be for Halloween that year,

I was instantly curious. I certainly didn't remember a superhero by that name from my cartoon-watching days, but I also knew I was not up to date with what kids my nephew's age were seeing. Wait a minute, did this officially mean I was *old*? Not quite. I actually got a preview of Ultimate Man earlier that fall when my family and I were on vacation. It turned out Ultimate Man and Captain America were one and the same.

I tried to ask my nephew what made Ultimate Man so ultimate. Was it his speed? His strength? His readiness to help people in need and fight for freedom and justice for all? Or was it just his super-cool costume and shield? As interested as I was to hear what my favorite little dude might say, I quickly learned that trying to have meaningful conversation with him at age four was futile. I got no response, so I can only assume it was all about the costume.

That same year my niece, who was about two and a half years old at the time, also was showing interest in superpowers—had we been wise enough to read the signs. She went through a phase where she would put her little hands on her hips and stomp her foot whenever she really wanted to do something. For example, with hands on hips and using her loudest voice, she would announce, "I want to go to the park *right now*!" This was followed by a stomp of her foot for extra emphasis. Every time I saw this behavior, I wondered where it came from. I had never seen my sister put her hands on her hips and stomp her foot as she insisted that her husband or the kids do something. Yet when I finally saw *Frozen* and watched Elsa make ice and snow for the first time, everything about my niece's unusual new behavior made sense. Watching that movie also explained why my niece was forever sticking her hand out in front of anyone who walked by her. She was trying to freeze us.

With these mysteries finally solved, I'm sure it will come as no surprise to learn that we had an Elsa along with our Ultimate Man at Halloween that year. In fact, Elsa returned the following Halloween. Joining her that year was Optimus Prime, who is the courageous hero and leader of the Autobots in the *Transformers* comic books, cartoon, and movies.

While traditional and modern superheroes are definitely fun, I think it's important to remember what the "superdogs" in that PowerPoint presentation I mentioned earlier were really trying to tell us. Superheroes don't need to wear flashy costumes, looking like they stepped straight from the silver screen or from the pages of a DC or Marvel comic book. Each of us can come as we are and make a pretty powerful impact just by using a combination of hard work and our natural talents to help others.

Maybe your superpower is teaching a child how to read, tie his or her shoes, ride a bike, or play a sport or a musical instrument. Maybe it's talking to the shy child in the neighborhood or to the one who looks different from everyone else. Your efforts to make kids like these feel comfortable could give them the confidence they need to make new friends. Maybe your superpower is helping an elderly neighbor with housework or just providing companionship throughout the week. Maybe it's volunteering each month at a nursing home or a soup kitchen. Maybe your superpower would inspire you to work at an animal shelter.

Sometimes it can be easy to figure out what your superpower is. Other times you may need a little help or inspiration. What's my superpower? I'm not sure I've discovered it yet. But I may be a little closer to figuring it out, thanks to some recent gifts I received from my family.

A couple of years ago as a belated Christmas-turned-birthday present, my sister gave me a plastic figurine of Tinker Bell. Since I'm a lifelong Disney fan, this was a delightful surprise. Peter Pan's spunky sidekick has always been one of my favorite characters. As a child watching the movie *Peter Pan*, I remember feeling a combination of awe and exhilaration when Tinker Bell held her wand at the ready and sprinkled the Darling children with pixie dust so they could fly. Well, if Wendy, Michael, and John could do it, why couldn't I? Tink sure looked like she had more than enough pixie dust to go around.

Of course, all those memories came back as soon as I saw my figurine. She stands near my laptop on the dining room table every day when I work from home. Her wand is held high in her right hand, looking like pixie dust is ready to shoot from its slightly bent tip at any moment. While I wished for the power to fly when I was a little girl, my adult self sometimes wishes my Tinker Bell could make my huge stack of work disappear or at least shrink a little bit. But as an adult, I remembered one thing about her magic that my younger self had been a little too enthralled to pay attention to. A spray of pixie dust from her wand wasn't enough for the magic to work. If you wanted to fly, you had to think wonderful thoughts first. The more I thought about this, I realized something else. Maybe Tink's powers didn't just stop with granting the ability to fly. Maybe she could inspire you to do anything if you believed with all your heart that you could. Maybe that's where her true magic comes from.

Faith, trust, and pixie dust can be good starting points when you need a little encouragement or motivation. But whatever your reason for needing some extra help, that assistance can come from sources that are much less magical.

I received two similarly inspiring gifts at Christmas in 2021. One came from my nephew. I was particularly excited to see what it would be because it came from his Secret Santa store at school. It was the first gift he had picked out just for me. His choice? A little red plastic car with a cluster of blue arrows on the hood and each door. One arrow in each group points straight ahead; the others also point ahead but slightly off to the left or right. When I asked my nephew why he'd gotten that for me, he told me he thought I would like it. He was right. The little car occupies a place of honor on the dining room table right near Tinker Bell and my laptop. When I look at it, it reminds me of two things. First, I am the only one in the driver's seat of my life. Second, no matter where you want to go in life, sometimes you have to take a bit of a detour to get there. Changing direction doesn't have to be a bad thing. It doesn't necessarily mean you're lost. Maybe going a different way shows you that there is more than one path to your goal, or it shows you possibilities you would have never considered otherwise. What's really important isn't how fast you go or which direction you take. It's that you never lose your drive until you reach your destination.

The third in this trio of special gifts was another plastic figurine, also from my sister. Now a Penn State Nittany Lion stands alongside Tinker Bell and the little red car. Since I'm a Penn State graduate and football fan, my sister knew this would be a great gift. While I'm sure this little lion will do his part to psych me up for every football season, he helps me in the off-season too. His enthusiastic expression cheers me on, no matter what task I'm trying to tackle. Perhaps most importantly, this little mascot reminds me that just like the teams he represents, I may not win at everything I do in life. But as long as I give my best effort, I will never truly lose.

No one ever said finding your superpower would be easy, and it might take a long time. But you get the idea. You don't have to be Wonder Woman or Superman to make a difference in the world. You'll never be able to solve problems with the wave of a magic wand. That doesn't mean you're powerless though. With some creative thinking, positive energy, determination, and courage, you are sure to find some ways to apply your natural gifts and talents to make a lasting impact in the lives of other people. You have the power to be a rainbow in someone's cloud anytime you choose, so why not get started today? No cape or pixie dust is required.

A Flash of Brilliance

Christmas has always been one of my favorite times of year. Whether it's the lights, the decorations, the tree, the music, the TV specials, the dinner, the cookies, or the presents, I love all the traditions associated with this holiday. In 2014 I was introduced to an activity that has since made its way onto my list of favorite things about the most wonderful time of the year: participating in a flash mob.

That got your attention, didn't it? What do Christmas and a flash mob have in common? We need to go back to my childhood to see the connection. Much like watching our football team win a state championship in 1992 was one of the happiest memories of my high school years, participating in the kazoo band was a standout experience from my time in elementary school. It was a rite of passage as the kazoo band was only open to fourth and fifth graders. It wouldn't surprise me to know that there were some students who wished they could have skipped right over kindergarten through third grade and headed straight for the kazoo big-time! This wasn't just any kazoo band, after all. It was the World

Famous Shaull School Kazoo Band. We had T-shirts *and* a banner that proclaimed our greatness. We gave assemblies at our school and a couple of other local elementary schools during the holiday season. What kids wouldn't want a taste of that as soon as they could get it? As if all of that wasn't enough to make students want to participate, the kazoo band was led by everyone's favorite teacher, Mr. Darr.

Any student in fourth or fifth grade could join the kazoo band. There were no special requirements and only a few rules. You had to remember your priorities: class first, kazoos second. Minimum grades were not required for kazoo band members, but you did have to come to class every day and give your best effort. With that said, woe to anyone who was stupid enough to try to play a kazoo in Mr. Darr's room when math or English class was in session. If you did that and were lucky, he would only confiscate it until class was over and warn you not to misbehave again. In the worst-case scenario, your kazoo would become intimately acquainted with the sole of one of Mr. D.'s steel-toed boots. This leads right into the second and third rules for participation: no screwing around in class (since school was your job at that age) and no behaviors that were mean or foolish, especially if they were dangerous or hurtful to a friend or another classmate. Those are pretty good rules for life well beyond age nine or ten, when you think about it.

Even on the rare occasions when Mr. Darr's temper flared, we knew it only happened because he cared so much about us and wanted the best for us. Many of his former students talk about what a great teacher he was and what an impact he made on their lives. I'll be the last person to dispute that. However, I think his greatest lessons were taught outside the classroom and had nothing to do with grammar, addition, subtraction, multiplication, or division. Here are some of the lessons I learned from Mr. D. that remain with me today:

1. Work hard and always try your best.
2. Rely on your brain to think for you, not a battery-powered device.
3. Always listen to your teacher.
4. Remember your manners and show respect to others.
5. When work is over, make plenty of time for fun, but be safe and responsible when you do. If you come away from the experience with a great story, so much the better!
6. Always be a friend and show kindness to others.
7. Don't exclude anyone. The sidelines of life can be a very lonely place.
8. Don't be afraid to try what you think you can't do. Whether it's solving a tough math problem or catching five football passes in a row to earn lunch at McDonald's, you can do what

you put your mind to if you keep a positive attitude and have a "coach" who believes in you.

9. Toot your own kazoo with joyful abandon, even if yours is the only blue kazoo in a sea of red ones. (This was the case for me during that first flash mob, but it was a vintage kazoo from my own days in the band. Just one example of how different can be good!)

10. Never miss a chance to give back and do something kind and unexpected for someone else when you can. The rewards will be far greater than you can imagine.

LESSONS LIKE THESE MAKE IT EASY TO SEE WHY Mr. Darr was one of the best-loved teachers in the school and why he still is. Naturally, when he put out a call to "his kids" on social media several years ago to help him realize his dream of reuniting the World Famous Shaull School Kazoo Band for a Christmas flash mob, there was never a question of how to respond. If you had a way to get there, you showed up. It wasn't just kazoo band alumni who got in on the fun either. Band members with their kids were part of the crowd too. Even some kazoo band parents came out to mark the start of this new tradition. Some just came to watch the festivities; others became honorary band members by playing a kazoo in honor of their children who couldn't make it back. Several of Mr. Darr's teaching colleagues were present too.

Even our former principal blew on a kazoo for what may have been the first time ever. I often say that words like *awesome*, *amazing*, and *epic* are way over-used. That was definitely not the case on December 20, 2014.

To the untrained ears of the busy shoppers who didn't realize what they were hearing, we probably sounded a lot like a swarm of angry bees buzzing tunelessly away. Maybe they even wished we would shut up and leave so they could wrap up their last-minute shopping in peace. But if they took a moment to stop and absorb what was happening, the sheer joy and delight on our faces would have been clear to see, as would the respect and love between students and their much-admired teacher. If they could spare a few minutes to stand still and really listen, they could hear the familiar tunes of "Silent Night," "Jingle Bells," and "We Wish You a Merry Christmas." For a brief time on that Saturday before Christmas, that special holiday magic took over, and we kazoo band members were carefree kids again, if only for about five minutes. Maybe we even brought smiles to the faces of some of those shoppers and took them back to simpler, happier times for a moment or two. I'd say that's a win-win situation.

Kazoo concerts always were eagerly anticipated in our grade school days, and the inaugural surprise performance held in the Capital City Mall food court was no exception. But that event was about far more than getting together to reminisce and play a few favorite Christmas songs on kazoo. It was, as our teacher pointed out to us after a brief practice session in the mall parking lot, about family, friends, and community. Even more than that, it was a shining example of the Christmas spirit. A group of people, some who knew one another and some who didn't, took a little time out of their jam-packed holiday schedules to get together to spread a bit of cheer in a world where it can often seem like there isn't much to be happy and hopeful about. In the process we got to help a beloved teacher and friend realize a long-held dream. Spreading joy, sharing love, and showing others you care—isn't that what Christmas is really all about?

It's said that good teachers never really stop teaching, even long after they turn out the lights in their classrooms for the last time. That day in December, Mr. D. didn't just give a crash course in kazooing for newbies or a refresher for rusty veterans. He didn't just teach us a fun Christmas-inspired routine to make us nostalgic for a more carefree time in our lives. I think he also was gently reminding us that Christmas is not always merry and bright for everyone. What about people who are alone or have recently lost a loved one? What if someone has recently lost a job and knows there can't be much under the tree? Maybe there can't even be a tree. I think Mr. Darr was encouraging us to remember that each of us can do something to make every day a little brighter for someone who needs it. If we all contribute in our own small way, that can add up to something really big. So what came together that day was more than a Christmas flash mob. It was a flash of brilliance that showed us how we could make things better for people in need any time of year, if we came together and made the effort. What a gift he gave us that day.

Was our pitch perfect? Hardly. Was our timing flawless? Nope. Did our dance moves make the cell phone videos that were taken go viral? Rest assured the internet was never in danger of breaking. But for about five minutes, we were all kids again, and we were spreading some Christmas cheer to people who may have needed it with our favorite teacher, who still loves us as much as we love him. I'd surely call that a flash of brilliance.

Now you may never have the opportunity to go to a mall five days before Christmas and participate in a flash mob kazoo concert. Only some of us can be so lucky! But maybe you can donate to a charity, work in a soup kitchen, help at an animal shelter, mentor a struggling teen, or spend time with an elderly neighbor who lives alone. All of these count as flashes of brilliance to me. They also could have the added benefit of keeping the Christmas spirit alive well past December 25. Maybe the light you create and share at Christmastime would even help you find a rainbow in the year to come and encourage you to share that light with others.

No Rainbows without Some Rain

I don't know anyone who isn't happy when they see a rainbow arcing across the sky. Did you know there is more to a rainbow than meets the eye? As *National Geographic* tells us, rainbows are actually full circles, not the arcs or half circles we recognize so easily. Only if you are at just the right spot on an airplane might you be lucky enough to see the full circle of a rainbow. Otherwise, people on the ground can only see the light that's reflected by raindrops above the horizon. Unless two people are exactly the same height and standing at the same vantage point, everyone's horizon is a bit different. This means most people will see a slightly different rainbow from that of their closest neighbor.

I started this book with a story about a rainbow, so it only seems fitting to bring things full circle with another rainbow story. If you think back to the original rainbow recipe I shared in my opening story, you remember that light is only one of the key ingredients. Let's also not forget that you can't have a rainbow without having some rain first. When I was a little girl, my mother would always tell me the same thing when I was dealing with a very sad or difficult situation. She would say, "Into each life some rain must fall." That was Mom's gentle way of reminding me that everyone had tough times. If we were lucky, they would pass quickly like a brief rain shower. Or they might stay a little longer, like an angry storm. Either way, though, they would not last forever. Besides, in its own way, some rain can be a good thing. If we can weather the challenging or sad times, we can appreciate the good ones even more. In other words if we want to experience the beauty of the rainbow, we have to learn to live with the rain first.

If you enjoy seeing rainbows as much as I do, I can think of no better place to do it than Hawaii. Hawaii's nickname of the Rainbow State is no accident. Its climate and geographic location are ideal for rainbows to form regularly. In fact, scientists who specialize in studying the atmosphere consider the islands of Hawaii the rainbow capital of the world. Especially during the rainy season, which lasts from November to April, it is a rare day on the islands that you won't see at least one rainbow. Kauai is reported as one of the best Hawaiian islands to see rainbows. Known as the Garden Isle because of its lush tropical vegetation, Kauai averages between thirty and forty inches of rain a year. This makes it prime rainbow-spotting territory.

How lucky, then, that I was able to visit this piece of paradise in February 2007, along with ten other family members. What a spectacular place for a vacation/family reunion, where three milestone birthdays also were celebrated during the week. Everything about the trip truly was unforgettable.

We enjoyed many fun activities during our stay on Kauai. Highlights included plenty of beach time, tours of the island by catamaran and helicopter, and a luau. When you go on a once-in-a-lifetime trip like this, souvenir shopping also makes your list of must-do activities.

To those who know me, it won't be surprising that I couldn't decide on just one souvenir from that vacation. Several special mementos were packed in my suitcase for the trip home. One of them was a vibrant blue short-sleeved T-shirt. On the front was a small drawing, all in white, of a stick figure with a mountain and a shining sun over one of its shoulders. The stick figure was standing under a rainbow that only included three stripes: one red, one yellow, and one blue. Written underneath the scene was a four-word phrase common in Hawaiian culture that reminds us that rainbows can't exist without rain to bring them to life. I'm sure the shirt's bright blue color was what caught my eye first. Not long after that, I noticed the drawing with its childlike simplicity. But what I found on the back of this T-shirt guaranteed it was coming home with me. Spoiler alert: that's saying a lot. I usually bypass T-shirts with a lot of writing on the back because I'm almost always in my wheelchair and no one can see my back.

It really is a shame that my back isn't visible when I wear this shirt. The back is the best part. Across the top is a heading that names a list of ten rules related to spending time on Kauai. When I first saw the list's title, I thought, *Wait a minute. Lots of people come to Hawaii on vacation. Vacations are supposed to be fun. Can't people take a break from rules then?* I soon realized I was overthinking, which I tend to do more than I usually like to admit. That was probably violating another major rule of Hawaiian life: Don't overanalyze the simple things. Sometimes it's OK just to enjoy something for what it is.

With that in mind, I focused on the list's contents rather than its title. As I look back on our vacation and that T-shirt, it seems to me that these rules don't just relate to vacationing or living on Kauai. These rules certainly could apply to anyone who wants to adopt a happier, more relaxed, more hopeful approach to life no matter where you call home. If this sounds good to you, let's take a closer look at each idea. The list below wasn't taken directly from the T-shirt. I've put each idea into my own words and added some of my own interpretation. I hope this will give you some insight into the aloha spirit and make it easier to accept that, at least in nature, rainbows can't come without some rain.

Decide to have a good day before you check the weather. People who live on Kauai have a saying about the weather. "If you don't like the weather, wait five minutes. It will change." Even though I only spent one week on the island, I found this to be accurate. I remember several afternoons when my family and I were sunbathing on the beach under a brilliant blue sky. We'd close our eyes for a few minutes to really relax and soak in the warmth and tranquility of our surroundings. The next thing we knew, we'd feel a sprinkling of raindrops. But this never sent us scrambling to pack our beach bags and head back to our time-share. Instead, it made us giggle with delight. We were on the beach during the last week of February. It was raining, but the sun was still out, and it really did last about five minutes. What's more, we saw a rainbow when we opened our eyes! Where else could this happen but Hawaii? And we were there!

One of the lessons from this judgment-free philosophy seems to be to live in the moment and appreciate whatever you have around you. Also, don't judge a day by something that's out of your control. Focus on what you can control, do the best you can, and the rest will take care of itself. If a rain cloud does move across your patch of sunlight, don't despair. Just wait. There's a good chance that your patience will be rewarded with something even more beautiful when the cloud passes.

People, much more than possessions, make life worth living. American culture places a fair amount of emphasis on acquiring things. We work to support ourselves and our families. If we're lucky, we also work because we have a passion for our chosen career. We tend to believe that we work hard, so we deserve the things we have. Why shouldn't we show off if we want to? We've earned it. What's more, some of us seem to think that the more possessions we have, the further ahead we are. Whether it's a bigger house, a faster car, or whatever latest, greatest thing we think we need to make us happy, it seems like some of us are always chasing something. If we acquire it, we may settle down for a while. Yet when the novelty and shine wear off, we are right back in the chase for the next big thing.

This rule reminds me of something one of my college professors shared with the class one day. She said that we tend to be so obsessed with getting more stuff that we transform from human beings, who simply enjoy and appreciate what they have, into human doings, who are so consumed with wanting more that they will do whatever it takes to get it. This viewpoint paints a gloomy picture, I know. It makes it seem like we Americans care far more about what we have in our lives than who we have in our lives. But I believe there's hope for our stuff-obsessed society. It seems like the older we get, the more we realize that our possessions aren't really as important as we once thought they were. Even now when I might be about halfway through my life, I look around at all the stuff I have accumulated and wonder what I'm going to do with it in a few months, much less years or decades from now. When I feel overwhelmed by that, I realize that what matters most is not how much I have but who I have to share it with. The best things in life aren't the things you acquire. Rather, the best parts of life are the people you care about and the memories you make with them. The imprint you leave on the hearts of those you love will last longer than any material object ever could.

Be honest—it's easier to keep your story straight. People may lie for any number of reasons. They may do it for harmful, self-serving reasons like wanting to control the outcome of a situation. Maybe the motivation for lying is to avoid punishment or embarrassment, either for ourselves or someone else. Lies might start out with the best of intentions, such as trying to protect another person we care about from hurt or disappointment. Whatever the reason for deceit, one thing seems to be true about all lies. What may start out as small and seemingly inconsequential can snowball out of control quickly. We start out telling one lie, and then we have to tell a string of others to cover up the original one. That can make it very hard to keep the story straight. One little slipup can bring the entire house of cards tumbling down, which may cause irreparable damage to a relationship. Telling the truth, on the other hand, is much easier on the memory and frees up space in the mind for more important things. It also helps strengthen the bonds of love and trust in a relationship. Over time, honesty helps turn a flimsy house of cards into a solid foundation that can withstand almost anything.

If you must speak loudly, let your clothes do the talking for you. Everyone won't always agree with you just because you have the loudest voice. Instead of supporting you, people may tell you to keep your opinion to yourself and leave them alone. They may not use such polite words though. On the other hand, when was the last time you heard someone criticize the "loudness" of another person's outfit, especially if the outfit included a Hawaiian shirt? I know if I see someone in a Hawaiian shirt—or in my case a Hawaiian dress—I'm going to wonder, *Where's the party? Is there room for one more?* While we were vacationing on Kauai, I noticed something about the shirts and dresses I saw on the tourists and in the souvenir shops. They included every color of the rainbow, which is so central to Hawaiian culture. To Hawaiians rainbows symbolize transformation and a connection between this world and the next one. With these ideas in mind, what could it be like if we incorporated more of these colors into our clothes and into our lives?

I'm not an artist or a psychologist, so I'm not going to talk about color theory or the personality traits that different colors represent. I'll just use an everyday example. Some colors clash. Think of an orange shirt paired with red pants. Most of us would never put those colors together as separate parts of the same outfit—at least not if we were going out in public. But no one would think twice about combining those colors with a bunch of others in a Hawaiian shirt. I've also never heard anyone question or criticize the colors in a rainbow or the way they're put together. People just appreciate the rainbow's beauty. How we see something depends on perspective and a willingness to think creatively about finding ways for things that don't seem to mesh to actually fit together well.

Just like colors, voices can clash from time to time. We can get so caught up in trying to make sure our opinions are heard that what may start as a pleasant conversation deteriorates into a shouting match. The din can become so overwhelming that our only goal is to drown the other people out rather than listening to what they have to say. If we speak more softly, though, something unexpected could happen. We might find that our ideas and opinions don't really clash so much after all. We might find ways that we could live and work together more peacefully and harmoniously.

The next time you have to express yourself, think about the best way you could do it. If you must speak loudly, try to make sure your message is positive, encouraging, and helpful. After you've made your point, be quiet so you can hear what others have to say. Leave the loudness to your shirt. You'll still make a lasting impression, and the overall effect will be much more positive.

Don't get so focused on a goal that you can't see anything else. Even expert archers miss the bull's-eye once in a while. If you widen your target area, your arrow will never miss. I don't think this rule is telling us to wander aimlessly through life, just going wherever we want to whenever we feel like it. Instead, I think it's telling us to stay open to new possibilities. You may achieve the goal you had in mind at the start of your journey, only to find out it wasn't everything you hoped it would be. You shouldn't be so hyperfocused on one goal that you miss other opportunities that could lead to something just as rewarding as (or even more so than) what you thought you wanted in the first place. Everyone doesn't always have clear goals in life. Sometimes you just have to shoot an arrow into the air and see where it lands. As long as no one is harmed by the shot, that can be OK. If you aim an arrow toward the moon and miss your target, you'll still end up among the stars.

Don't worry so much about what you accumulate during your lifetime. You can't take it with you at the end. In your last moments on the earth, you probably won't be wondering why you didn't upgrade to a better smartphone when you had the chance. You're more likely to be thinking, *I'd give anything to stay here and watch my grandchildren grow up,* or *I wish I could say "I love you" to my husband (or wife) one more time.* When your family and friends gather to mourn your passing, they won't be upset that you didn't have a bigger TV or a faster car with more bells and whistles. The stuff you spent a lifetime accumulating won't matter in the end. You can't take it with you wherever you end up, and your loved ones may not want most of it either. After my maternal grandfather passed away several years ago, my mother and her two siblings had to deal with the monumental task of cleaning out the house. The conversations that took place when the three of them were sorting through their parents' belongings usually went something like this:

"Do you want this?"

"No. You take it."

"No, you can have it."

"No. Really, it's OK. I'd rather you have it."

I couldn't begin to tell you how many of these exchanges took place in the days following my grandfather's funeral. My mother and her brother and sister led the way on this topic, but we grandchildren felt much the same way. Most of the things that were left behind just didn't mean as much to us as they had to my grandparents. We kept a few pieces of furniture, some of my grandmother's jewelry and knickknacks, and a few special mementos my grandfather had treasured. But what we really wanted—what we would have given anything in that house to have—was more time with Granny and Pop-Pop. So make that visit. Go on that adventure. Do whatever you've been waiting to do, if you're able. Tell those closest to you how much they mean. Keep old stories alive and make new memories while you still can. This is the legacy that will last, not the possessions you leave behind.

Age is just a number. But it seems to get bigger faster every year. Time is a funny thing. It seemed to stretch on forever when we were kids, especially when we were looking forward to something. Whether it was a sleepover at our best friend's house, going trick-or-treating, or just a regular weekend, time seemed to slow to a crawl the closer we got to the event. The last few weeks of school before summer vacation always took forever. Let's not forget about waiting for our birthday each year to see if someone came through with that special present we wanted. That can be sheer agony for a little boy or girl. When we become adults, though, what felt like forever seems to fly by in the blink of an eye. Every time my niece or nephew has another birthday,

I think, *Wait. Didn't I just get home from the hospital after holding you for the first time? Stop growing up so fast!* Every time a holiday comes around, I look at my calendar and wonder where the year is going. Didn't the ball just drop in Times Square?

The older we get, the more precious time becomes. Live every day to the fullest. Make the most of your opportunities. Don't rush through any phase of life. Time will make each chapter of your life story seem too short anyway. The good experiences you have right now may never come again, so savor them. Remember that every day you get to wake up is a fresh start, a chance to improve on the day before. You get twenty-four hours to use as you will. You can waste them or do something positive for someone else or for yourself. How you spend each day matters because you are exchanging a day in your life for the use of that time. If tomorrow comes—which is never promised—find some reason to be happy.

Also, remember that the previous day is gone forever. There are no do-overs. In place of that day, you can leave a rain cloud or a rainbow. I know which one I would choose. What about you? Even though your body may feel old when you make it past the crest of the hill and start the downward slide, try to stay young at heart and grateful for the time you've been given. When you get to the bottom of your hill, don't say, "Whew! Thank goodness that's over." Instead, opt for something like "What a ride! Thanks for the sunshine and the rain, and especially the rainbows!"

You can be rich in one of two ways: earn more money or learn to live with fewer things. The first definition of *richness* is straightforward. It's easy enough to understand that someone who earns $200,000 a year is considered richer than someone who earns $50,000. The person who is more financially well off generally will have a larger, more nicely furnished home; a higher-end car; and many of the other status symbols we associate with tangible wealth, including more money saved in the bank. Even if we are lucky enough to have plenty of money available, that doesn't guarantee that we protect it for the future. Instead of putting more money away for the rainy days ahead, we may be tempted to live beyond our means. Whether you are a spender or a saver, a bigger bank account doesn't guarantee long-term wealth or financial security. Your fortune can change in the blink of an eye. Just ask someone who suddenly loses a job or anyone who invests in the stock market.

Maybe it's a good idea to consider a different definition of *wealth*. If we allow ourselves to become driven by wanting more all the time, we may become so consumed by that desire to show off our wealth that we end up being eaten alive by it. Our constant hunger for more will never be satisfied, no matter how much stuff we accumulate. Instead of being in a hurry to buy more things to flaunt our earning power, we should take more time to appreciate what we have and take care of it so it lasts. If we can truly value what we have, whether it's a little or a lot, we will find that we have an embarrassment of riches.

Real beauty comes from the inside. Looks don't mean much. Of all the rules on the list, this one surprised me the most at first. Hawaii is one of the most beautiful places I've ever visited. There is external beauty everywhere. When our family got together for breakfast during our first morning on Kauai, I remember crying for two reasons. First, I was so happy to see my family. Most of us don't see one another very often because we live so far apart. The other reason for my tears was that I was overwhelmed to be in such a beautiful place with so many people I love. Everywhere I looked was a postcard view. It was impossible not to be emotional about the breathtaking beauty that surrounded us. External beauty had to count for something on an island like Kauai.

After thinking about this latest rule, I realized that the original author of this list was talking about people when he said looks mean nothing and real beauty is internal. The people who live on Kauai are hardly unattractive, though, whether they are lifelong island residents or transplants from the mainland. Looking back, though, I think the most attractive thing about them wasn't their appearance. It was their warm, friendly personalities and their laid-back approach to life. Still, I can definitely appreciate the deeper wisdom here. We should be careful not to get sucked in by a pair of beautiful eyes, a bright smile, or a nice figure. In time our bodies will become softer and weaker. Our hair will thin and turn gray. We may even lose a tooth or two. But our hearts will show our true beauty even when our bodies start to let us down. If we can always love, appreciate, and treat one another with kindness, dignity, and respect, we can be just as beautiful at ninety-two as we were at twenty-two—probably even more so.

There are no rainbows without some rain. Unless you are lucky enough to live on a Hawaiian island or some other piece of tropical paradise, you may not get to see rainbows very often. When rainbows do appear, they typically don't remain in the sky for long. Each one I've seen has only lasted a few minutes. Rainbows may be fleeting, but I have never known anyone who doesn't enjoy seeing one. A rainbow never fails to make me smile and feel more hopeful regardless of what struggle or sadness I may be facing at the time. No matter how much happiness and hope rainbows bring, though, they could never be made without two very important ingredients: rain and sunlight. The clouds and rain must come first if a rainbow is to appear later. Then we must be patient and wait for the sun to come out if we want to be rewarded with a rainbow. It's that way in life too.

Every day is not going to be bright and sunny with not a cloud in the sky. Some gray, cloudy skies may bring showers that barely dampen your spirit. Other clouds may be dark and foreboding, seeming to stretch along the entire horizon. They may unleash torrents of rain that threaten to wash away everything in their path. You may even feel like you're going to drown from the intensity of the deluge. But if you remain patient and keep looking up, you'll see that the rain will stop, the clouds will break, and the light will shine through to create the rainbow you've been waiting for. Soak that rainbow in when you see it. Save the light to recharge yourself when you need it, and also share some with others who are weathering their own showers or storms. When the storms are over, never stop seeing rainbows through the clouds.

About the Author

A LIFELONG PENNSYLVANIA RESIDENT, PAULA Marinak has always enjoyed reading and writing. She graduated from Penn State Harrisburg in 2002 with a communications degree. After college, she worked as an editor for three years until her career path took a turn. She has worked in human resources since 2006, but has always held on to her dream of writing a book thanks to the encouragement of family, friends and a former elementary school teacher. In her free time, Paula enjoys anything involving her beloved yellow Lab Rosie and her fur niece – a golden retriever named Penny – whether taking a walk, teaching a new trick or behavior, or enjoying some cuddle time. Paula also enjoys watching college sports, especially football and men's basketball. She and her pack live in the Harrisburg area.

PHOTO CREDIT: CARISA KOZICKI

9 798822 905283